GhostHunter
Walks in Kent

Rupert Matthews

S.B. Publications

First published in 2005 by S. B. Publications
Tel: 01323 893498
Email: sbpublications@tiscali.co.uk

ISBN 1-85770-300-6

Designed and Typeset by EH Graphics (01273) 515527

Front cover photo: *Hothfield Church, Rochester Castle and Kits Coity House*
Back cover photo: *Leeds Castle*

Contents

The author

GhostHunter Walks in Kent

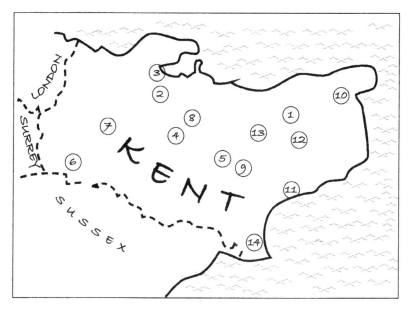

1	Canterbury	8	Hollingbourne
2	Blue Bell Hill	9	Hothfield
3	Rochester & Chatham	10	Minster
4	Leeds Castle	11	Saltwood
5	Pluckley	12	Bridge
6	Penshurst	13	Chilham
7	West Peckham	14	Romney Marsh

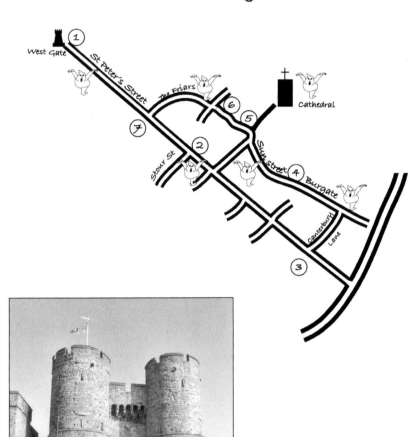

Walk No.1
Canterbury

West Gate

St Peter's Street

The Friars

Cathedral

Stour St

Sun Street

Burgate

Canterbury Lane

1
2
3
4
5
6
7

The West Gate of Canterbury, where the walk starts.

Canterbury

Distance:	**1.5 miles**
Ghostly Rating:	*** * * * * * * ***
Route:	**Central Canterbury**
Map:	**OS Explorer 150**
Start/Parking:	**West Gate, Canterbury**
Public Transport:	**The city of Canterbury is at the centre of several bus routes and has two railway stations.**
Conditions:	**This walk is entirely over city centre streets, most of them pedestrianised.**
Refreshments:	**There are numerous pubs, cafes, restaurants and snackbars along the route of this walk and in central Canterbury.**

This is a short, gentle walk around the city centre of Canterbury. There is, of course, much to see and do in Canterbury other than ghosthunting, and there are numerous signposts to show the visitor the way to the castle, abbey and other historic sights that are not on this walk.

The Walk

1) From the West Gate, walk southeast into St Peter's Street. This pedestrianised thoroughfare is the oldest in Canterbury, following the route of the main street of the Roman city. The imposing gabled house on your right is the Old Weaver's House.

This building is, in fact, not one house but several. They were built as a terrace in the later 16th century by Huguenot refugees fleeing persecution in France. They brought with them their skills as weavers, setting up their looms in the upper storeys of these houses and running shops from the ground floor. It is these looms that account for both the name of the building and for the windows, unusually large for domestic buildings of this date. The business of weaving needed good natural light.

Quite what accounts for the haunting is less clear. The shadowy figure of a lady in a long dress has been seen walking up one of the staircases on several occasions. She is rather indistinct, so it is difficult to be precise about the period from which she dates. Whoever she is, and however long she has been here, she is a gentle soul who goes about her business ignoring the mortal world around her.

2) Continue along St Peter's Street. After it passes Stour Street on the right, the road

High Street, Canterbury, plays host to a phantom mayor.

becomes the High Street.

The High Street and the narrow lanes off it have in recent years been the site of several sightings of a mysterious figure on a bicycle. Several pedestrians have been forced to leap out of the way of a cyclist who swoops around corners without regard for those in his way. Some have merely muttered under their breath about thoughtless road users, but others have turned to watch the miscreant only to see him vanish before their eyes.

Exactly who this man might be is unknown. He is smartly dressed, though his suit is said to be rather old fashioned in some undefined way, and his head is bare. These features might date him to some time in the later 1960s or 1970s, but even that is uncertain. All that can be said, with certainty, is that it is best to get out of the way of speeding cyclists in Canterbury High Street. Be they mortal or phantom, it is wise not to risk a collision.

3) Where the High Street ceases to be pedestrianised, turn left into Canterbury Lane. At the far end of this short lane, turn left again into Burgate.

The ghost of Burgate is another of Canterbury's often seen but remarkably elusive figures. When he appears, he is visible clearly enough. The phantom bustles down the street apparently in some hurry to get to where he is going and giving every appearance of impatience and fussing. He is dressed in a long pale cloak, so it is generally thought that he is a monk or clergyman from centuries past. What his mission might be and why he feels the need for haste are quite unknown.

4) Where this lane bears right it becomes Sun Street.

The spectral events of Sun Street are far more precise than those met so far on this walk, but unfortunately they no longer occur. Standing at the side of the road is an ancient pump which brought up water from deep underground for the convenience of residents in this street. In these days of mains water supply it is no longer needed, and has been blocked off for fear of visitors drinking polluted water.

Back in the days when it was used by Canterbury residents, however, the pump of Sun Street was famous for the fact that, now and then, the water it supplied would suddenly run as red as blood. It was generally believed that this was a miraculous event linked to the blood of the saint and martyr, St Thomas Becket, which had seeped into the ground as he lay dying in the cathedral. The waters were bottled and sold to pilgrims, as well as being accounted lucky to use for bathing.

5) At the end of Sun Street the lane opens out into a small square with a tall cross at its centre. On the right is the entrance to the cathedral.

There are a number of phantoms linked to the cathedral. Easily the most famous is the phantom monk who lurks in the crypt. This figure is said to be the ghost of St Thomas Becket, one time Archbishop of Canterbury and patron saint of the city.

Becket was born the son of an English merchant in London in about 1118 and sent to Merton Priory to be educated. There he left his father's trade and instead applied himself to learning the intricacies of managing the households of the wealthy and to learning court etiquette. In 1142 he gained the post of private secretary to Theobold, Archbishop of Canterbury, and in 1155 was poached by the new King, Henry II, to join his household. Becket proved to be as devoted to the king as he had been to the Archbishop and his skill at finances quickly led to his promotion to being Chancellor of England. In 1162, Theobold died and Henry persuaded the Pope to install Becket as the new Archbishop. Henry hoped that Becket would alter Church policy on matters of dispute with the Crown in favour of the Crown.

Sun Street, scene of a haunting from days gone by.

Becket, however, now proved loyal to his new employer, the Church and refused to do a deal with Henry. The king was furious and England plunged into turmoil as barons, bishops and commoners took sides in the dispute between King and Archbishop. The centre of the dispute was who administered justice in England. Henry believed that, ultimately, it was the king's justice that should prevail. The laws he passed and the common laws should apply to everyone in the kingdom, who should be judged in courts set up by the king. Becket, however, maintained that clergy and Church lands came under the laws of God, which were authorised by the Pope and administered by the clergy. Not only were the two law codes quite different, an act being a crime under one but not the other, but there were numerous opportunities for confusion. For instance, if a commoner committed a crime on Church lands it was not entirely clear which court had jurisdiction. The dispute soon widened to touch on taxation and broader concepts of loyalty. In some ways it was a dispute between the flexible, common law of England that had been built up over centuries of experience and the continental system of fixed, written laws.

The murder of Archbishop Thomas Becket has left its ghostly mark in Canterbury, and elsewhere in Kent.

In 1164 Becket left to consult the Pope in Rome on the legal aspects of the matter. While he was away, Henry reached a compromise with the other bishops in England. Becket promptly excommunicated the bishops and ordered that they resign their offices immediately. The dispute rumbled on until December 1170 when a knight from King Henry's household was caught hunting without permission on Church lands. Becket at once hauled the man before a Church court for trial. When Henry heard that his friend had been convicted and sentenced in a Church court without so much as a by your leave, he flew into a terrible rage. "Will nobody rid me of this turbulent priest?" demanded the king, whereupon four knights rode to Canterbury and on 29 December murdered the archbishop in his own cathedral on the steps of the altar in the chapel of St Benedict.

Henry had to atone for his part in the killing, promising to respect Church laws and Church revenues. Thomas was quickly canonised by the Pope he had served so well, and his shrine in Canterbury Cathedral became the most magnificent in England. His cult was the centre for pilgrimages from all over northern Europe, and the cathedral at Canterbury was rebuilt in its current magnificent style using the money brought in by pilgrims. The shrine was torn down in the Reformation, but the ghost of Becket remains.

A second ghost in the cathedral area is that of a second archbishop. This is Simon Sudbury and, like Becket before him, he came to a violent and bloody end. Unlike Becket, however, Sudbury was a loyal servant to his king, in this case King Richard II. Sudbury was the chief finance minister and it was largely his idea that the king levied a tax that had to be paid by every adult in the country. The tax was levied on a sliding scale with noblemen paying a pound and peasants two pennies, but it was a heavy tax and a new tax. The people did not

Canterbury Cathedral towers over the city and is the focus of some odd supernatural activity.

like it. They liked it even less when the tax was collected yet again in 1380.

In 1381 Archbishop Sudbury inspected the rolls detailing how much money had been raised. He noticed that in Kent, Essex and a few other counties much less money had been collected than previously. He sent a new set of tax collectors out to check the figures of the first lot. For the peasants of Kent, it was too much. They believed that an entirely new tax was being collected and rose in rebellion. On 10 June the peasants marched into Canterbury under the leadership of a workman named Wat Tyler. They broke into Sudbury's Palace to seize the tax rolls, but Sudbury had fled to London and taken his rolls with him.

Undaunted the peasants marched on London, being joined by thousands of others from Essex, Surrey and other counties. The peasants marched to oppose heavy taxation, to set rents at a reasonable level and to free labourers and workmen from onerous restrictions on their work. The men poured into London and acted with great restraint. They had come to right wrongs, not to plunder or loot. They did, however, exact a bloody vengeance on Archbishop Sudbury. He was dragged out by Wat Tyler and beheaded in front of a cheering crowd.

Soon afterward Tyler was himself killed by the Mayor of London after an argument. The peasants dispersed to their homes after being promised everything they had demanded. King Richard later ordered the execution of the ringleaders and broke most of his promises, but many of the peasants' demands came to fruition in the years that followed.

Also making its first appearance in the wake of the Peasants' Revolt was the ghost of Archbishop Sudbury. The ghost was seen, and recognised, by those who knew him. It appeared in the long, warm grey cloak that the Archbishop habitually wore when off duty and was seen most often in or near the Sudbury Tower, where he had had his private chambers and offices. To this day the Archbishop's ghost is prone to appear around the Sudbury Tower, dressed in his comfortable old cloak. Perhaps he feels at home.

Within the cathedral precincts stands the King's School, occupying land and buildings that in Sudbury's day were occupied by the monastery attached to the cathedral. The door that gives access to the school from the cathedral precincts is a potentially dangerous spot that goes by the name of the Dark Entry.

Back in the 18th century there was a servant girl named Nell Cook at the school who waited on the masters and cleaned their rooms. She fell in love with one of the masters, who was also a clergyman. This man did not return Nell's affections and turned her down on the grounds that he was a man of the cloth with his thoughts on matters altogether more spiritual. Nell was disappointed, but consoled herself with the belief that her lover was dedicating himself to higher matters.

It was with understandable fury and feelings of betrayal, therefore, that Nell discovered her supposed saintly lover in bed with another woman just a few days later. In fury, Nell killed them both and then herself. The poor girl was hurriedly buried beneath the flagstones of the school, close to what is now the Dark Entry.

Her ghost appeared soon afterwards, and has been glimpsed frequently ever since. This is not a ghost that it is wise to approach. She is pretty enough, but her features are contorted with grief and rage. There is an indefinable air of disturbance and malice when she appears. Those who see her are often upset and have trouble sleeping for some time thereafter. Poor Nell is said to bring bad luck, one version of her story has it that she foretells death within a year and a day in the family of those who see her. Poor Nell.

6) Leaving the cathedral precincts, bear right into Orange Street. At the end of Orange Street cross Kiln Street to enter The Friars. You will soon come across Marlowe Theatre.

The phantom of the Marlowe Theatre is more recent than most of the others in Canterbury, having been seen for the first time only in 1967. Dressed casually in slacks and a jumper, the phantom was at first taken to be some fan or other intruder who had somehow gained access to the backstage area. After a few fruitless searches for the supposed intruder, he was accepted as a ghost. Whenever he appeared after that, lounging in the wings or wandering slowly down a corridor, he was simply ignored. As he is to this day.

7) At the far end of The Friars, turn right back into St Peter's Street. The West Gate is straight in front of you.

Archbishop Sudbury as he would have appeared when conducting services in his beloved cathedral.

Becket fell here.

Cathedral nave.

Road by cathedral gate.

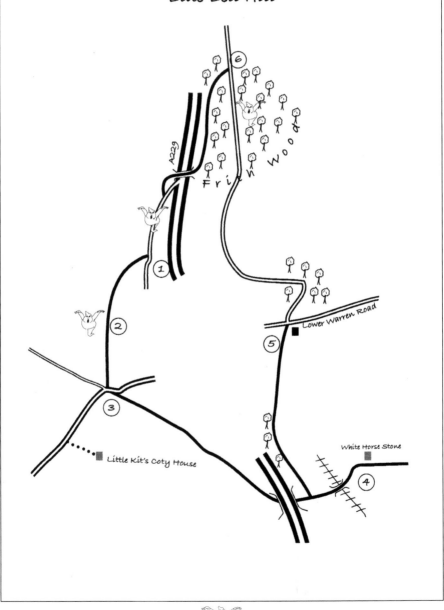

Walk No.2
Blue Bell Hill

Blue Bell Hill

Distance:	2.5 miles
Ghostly Rating:	****
Route:	Around Blue Bell Hill
Map:	OS Explorer 148
Start/Parking:	Parking is available in the side road at the foot of Blue Bell Hill.
Conditions:	This route is largely over well-maintained byways and bridlepaths.
Refreshments:	There are no refreshments available on this walk.

Stamina and the ability to scramble up and down steep hills is called for on this short walk, but the effort is repaid with sweeping views from the North Downs south over central Kent and the valley of the River Medway. The ghosts are a disturbing lot, ranging from the truly terrifying to the barbarian.

The Walk

1) Park in the side road at the foot of Blue Bell Hill. Take the A229 south from Rochester, leaving at the slip road signposted to "Eccles" and "Burham". Follow the slip road as it curves to the right and passes under the A229. Turn right immediately past the bridge and park near the top of the hill, where a footpath sign to the left indicates the way to "Kit's Coty House".

This stretch of road is possibly the most famous haunted highway in England, certainly it is well known in Kent. The spectre represents the supernatural at its most terrifying. Not that she appears all that frightening at first sight.

The ghost of Blue Bell Hill is a rather attractive young lady with long blonde hair. She stands by the side of the road and

The old road down Blue Bell Hill which has seen more phantom encounters than most other stretches of road in Kent.

jerks her thumb at passing cars as if seeking a lift from drivers. Some motorists have stopped, which has been their first mistake. Exactly what happens next varies between witness accounts, but all are agreed it is a quite terrifying experience.

Some drivers report that as they slow down the young woman leaps out in front of their cars, running forward as if intent on causing collision. They brake sharply or swerve, only for the woman to vanish into thin air an instant before impact. Others say that they pull up next to the girl, only for her to transform slowly into a twisted old hag who exudes a feeling of intense evil and malice before running off into the woods. Perhaps most bizarre of all are the few who actually pick up the young girl, only to find that she vanishes abruptly once in the car.

Now that the modern A229 bypasses this stretch of road, the reports of this terrifying phantom have become much rarer. But you might be lucky – or unlucky depending on how you look at it.

The path off Bluebell Hill that runs down a steep flight of steps towards Kit's Coty House.

2) Take the footpath to the left signposted to "Kit's Coty House". This path runs downhill between an avenue of trees, the branches of which meet overhead creating a gloomy, atmospheric walk on even the brightest of days. After about 200 yards a break in the trees on the right opens into a sweeping hillside pasture, in which stands the tumbled megalithic monument that is today known as Kit's Coty House.

Kit's Coty House is, in reality, all that remains of a burial mound built some 5,000 years ago by the Neolithic farmers who then inhabited Kent. The covering mound of earth has long since worn away, leaving the standing stones and the capstone that once formed the burial chamber itself.

The ghosts here have nothing to do with the ancient farmers who erected Kit's Coty House, but date back a mere 1,500 years to the time when the English were invading what was then post-Roman Britain. Led by the brothers Hengist and Horsa, a force of English warriors landed at Ebbsfleet (see Walk No 10) to act as mercenaries for the post-Roman government. In the year 455 Hengist and Horsa led their English warriors in rebellion against their employers, sending word to their homeland in what is now Germany asking for reinforcements.

For a while the war raged back and forth, but reached a climax here on the south-facing slopes of the North Downs. An important Roman road ran down the slope here, while a second ran along the crest of the ridge just to the north. The River Medway, as it flows along the valley here, was both a trade route and a barrier, while the gap it cut in the North Downs had strategic importance. This was a crucial spot for the invading English armies and the forces that opposed them. Perhaps it was for this reason that Kit's Coty House was chosen as the venue for a single combat between Horsa and Vortigern, leader of the Romano-Britons. At stake was Kent – winner take all.

Kit's Coty House, scene of an ancient haunting.

The rival armies spread out on the slopes above Kit's Coty House from where they could gain a clear view of the combat to come. Dressed in their finest armour and carrying the best weapons the age could create, the champions came out on to the green downland turf to fight for the future of Kent. The fight was long and hard, epic enough to have inspired poetry. In the end Horsa was killed. Hengist and his English carried away their fallen hero and retreated to offshore islands, such as Thanet, Sheppey and Grain. They would be back. In 488 Hengist's son Oisc became independent King of Kent, and within a short period of time what is now England had been overrun by the invaders.

Meanwhile, Kit's Coty House had become the focus for a dramatic haunting. The ghosts of both Horsa and Vortigern returned to refight the battle that had, temporarily at least, decided the fate of Kent. They return here still, appearing as shadowy, half-transparent figures wielding shields, swords and spears as they thrust and hack at each other. The fight rages for a few seconds, then the figures gradually fade to nothing before any decision is reached.

3) Return to the footpath and continue downhill until it reaches a three-ways junction of country lanes. If you are interested you can walk straight on to reach Little Kit's Coty House. As its name suggests, this is a smaller version of the monument just visited, but no ghost story is attached to it. Otherwise, take the footpath that leads off diagonally left. This is part of the North Downs Way and is signposted as such, and as the Pilgrims Way. Follow this path through some trees, then over an open field to pass under the A229 through a subway.

4) Just beyond the A229 the path meets a well-surfaced byway at a T-junction. Turn right and cross the footbridge over a deep railway cutting in which runs the Channel Tunnel rail link. Just beyond the bridge, on the left, is the ancient White Horse Stone.

This is the ancient standing stone known for centuries as the White Horse Stone. Archaeological digs in the area, which took place before the rail tunnel and cutting were constructed to service the Channel

The death of the English leader Horsa at Kit's Coty House was to have a lasting impact on English history.

Tunnel, found evidence of Neolithic farming settlements dating back some 5,000 years. This would make the settlement about the same age as the burial mounds at Kit's Coty and Little Kit's Coty.

Local legend has it that after he was killed at Kit's Coty, the body of Horsa was brought here for burial by his grieving brother Hengist. The body was buried

The tumbled ruins of Little Kit's Coty House.

according to the pagan customs of the early English. Then Hengist painted the stone blood red and on it drew the figure of a prancing white horse. The symbol was taken up by Hengist's son Oisc and so became the symbol of the Kings of Kent, and is still used by the Kent County Council and other bodies representing the county that was once a kingdom.

5) Return back over the footbridge and continue straight on along the byway, ignoring the turning on the left by which you arrived. The byway goes uphill to reach a lane named Lower Warren Road. Cross Lower Warren Road to join a lane heading steeply uphill. Follow this lane as it bends left, then right, crosses open country and then plunges into a dense wood as it reaches the crest of the hill.

This is Frith Wood, and it is as well to tread carefully here. Something very big and very hairy has its lair here, though nobody knows quite what it is. Walkers and motorists on the lane have reported seeing a strange, large creature. It has been reported variously as a gorilla, a leopard, a bear or a lion, but all agree that it moves on all fours and can run very quickly indeed. Whether it is some creature escaped from a zoo or some spectral monster is not entirely clear. Best to take care.

6) Shortly before the lane leaves the wood, a footpath turns off on the left. Take this path steeply downhill to reach the edge of the A229. Follow the path alongside the road for a short distance until it reaches a footbridge. Cross the A229 by way of this footbridge, turning south along the lane beyond to return to the start point.

The entrance to the Pilgrims Way at the foot of Blue Bell Hill.

The lane through Frith Wood where a mysterious something has startled walkers.

The path that leads from Frith Wood back to Blue Bell Hill.

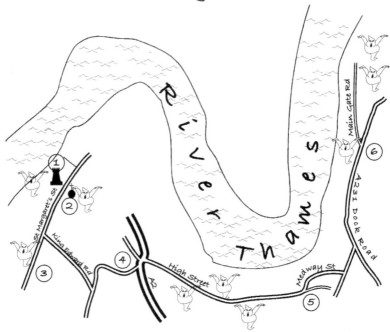

Walk No.3
Rochester & Chatham

The ghost of Rochester's most famous citizen haunts the spot where he wanted to be buried.

Rochester and Chatham

Distance:	2.5 or 5 miles
Ghostly Rating:	* * * * * * *
Route:	Rochester - Chatham - Rochester
Map:	OS Explorer 163
Start/Parking:	Rochester Castle
Public Transport:	Both Rochester and Chatham have railway stations, while both towns are served by several bus routes.
Conditions:	This walk is exclusively over town streets, so the surface is solid and useable in even the wettest weather.
Refreshments:	The walk includes a haunted pub, which offers good meals, and there are other cafes and shops selling snacks along the route.

This walk around Rochester and Chatham takes in the town centres of both towns, now almost run together, and embraces some historic sights. It is a relatively short and undemanding walk with only a couple of short hills of no great steepness. The pavements are well maintained and there is little difficulty finding your way. Parking can be difficult on Saturdays, so that day is best avoided for this walk unless you are arriving by public transport.

The Walk

1) The main entrance to Rochester Castle is through an ancient archway off The Esplanade, close to where that riverside road meets the A2 on the south side of the bridge over the Medway.

Civil War came to Rochester in 1264, causing a haunting that has persisted ever since.

King Henry III ran a corrupt government in which favoured courtiers helped themselves to the wealth of the kingdom and justice was available only to those who could bribe the right official. The situation was made worse by the fact that many of those lining their pockets so dishonestly were the French relatives of Henry's queen, Eleanor of Provence. In 1258 the nobles of England met in solemn conference at Oxford and, inspired by Simon de Montfort the Earl of Leicester, they drew up rules to ensure fair, honest government and forced Henry to sign them. In 1264 Henry hired an army of French mercenaries and repudiated his agreement. War broke out.

Rochester Cathedral has a gentle phantom who potters about.

Rochester Castle was held for the king by Sir Ralph de Capo, who had with him in the castle his betrothed, the beautiful Lady Blanche de Warrenne. Earl Simon moved to besiege Rochester and among his army was one Sir Gilbert de Clare. As ill fortune would have it, Lady Blanche had previously been betrothed to Sir Gilbert, but had broken off the engagement due to his violent temper.

After a siege of some weeks, Earl Simon learned that King Henry was at Lewes with an army much smaller than his own. Sensing a likely victory, Earl Simon abandoned the siege and marched off towards Lewes. As the army marched away, Sir Ralph sallied out to harry his enemies and recover what he could in the way of looted livestock and the like. Seeing this, Sir Gilbert led a small force that battered their way into Rochester Castle, slamming the gates behind them and declaring the castle now held for Earl Simon.

Sir Ralph, at once, rode back toward the castle, but it was too late. He arrived to see his beloved Lady Blanche high on the battlements of the keep fending off the unwanted advances of Sir Gilbert. Without hesitating, Sir Ralph put a bolt into his crossbow and sent it flying at Sir Gilbert. The bolt, however, glanced off Sir Gilbert's armour and instead struck Lady Blanche. The unfortunate lady died within seconds.

It is the phantom of Lady Blanche who returns to the battlements of Rochester Castle. She appears with long, flowing dark hair which waves gently in a summer's breeze, no matter what the actual weather may be. Her long, pale gown flutters loosely as she paces back and forth along the battlements. She usually appears for only a few seconds at a time, but often enough for there to be no doubt about her presence.

The topmost turret of Rochester Castle saw a fatal tragedy that has led to a persistent haunting.

2) Leave the castle by the way you entered, turning sharp right up a steep, narrow lane named Bakers Walk. At the top of the hill bear right around the castle walls into St

Margaret's Street. Rochester Cathedral is on the left.

Just as persistent as the phantom Lady Blanche is the genial old gent who potters about the burial ground of Rochester Cathedral, over the road from the castle. This elderly man in a dark suit is seen walking quietly around as if searching for something. He is, in fact, searching for his own tomb. He searches in vain for it is in Westminster Abbey, not here. The ghost is none other than Charles Dickens, the great Victorian novelist. Dickens grew up in Rochester in grinding poverty. At the age of 11 he was put to work in a factory, earning just six shillings per week to help the family finances. As he walked to work each morning, Dickens passed a fine house at Gad's Hill, Rochester, which he thought the most lovely in the world. In 1857 he bought it with money earned by his writing and lived there until his death in 1870.

As he lay dying, Dickens asked to be buried here, but a grateful nation decided to give him a grander burial in London instead. No wonder he returns here to search for his tomb. Presumably he is unhappy that his final wishes were not respected. The phantom Dickens is seen quite often, but never for very long. He ducks out of sight within seconds of being seen.

Lady Blanche de Warrenne, whose phantom lurks in Rochester Castle.

The cathedral itself is one of the oldest in England. It was founded in 604 by St Augustine, the first Archbishop of Canterbury. That early church burned down in the 11th century and was replaced by a massive Norman-style building which was extended in the 13th century to create the church as it stands today, give or take a bit of Victorian work.

3) Leave the cathedral and turn left, walking south along St Margaret's Street with the castle on your right. About 150 yards south of the castle stands the Cooper's Arms public house on the right.

A visitor from 800 years ago still pops in to the Cooper's Arms to make sure that all is well.

The Cooper's Arms is one of the oldest secular buildings in Rochester. It was built in the 14th century as the cooperage, where the barrels were made and repaired, for the Benedictine monastery that then occupied this area of the town.

The phantom is the shade of one of the medieval monks who used to frequent the building. For some reason he is seen only in the autumn, and then usually only once or twice each year. His appearance is, however, dramatic enough to make up for its infrequency. He walks into the bar by striding through a solid wall, where there was once a doorway. Having thus startled anybody in the bar at the time, the phantom monk looks around with distinct disapproval before turning around and returning whence he came.

Whether the ghostly monk disapproves of the secular use to which the old building is now put, or if he disapproves of something that existed here when he was alive, nobody can tell.

4) Leaving the Cooper's Arms, turn left, then right down King Edward Road. At the bottom of King Edward Road, turn left, following this road round to the right, then the left to reach a complex five-ways road junction. Cross the main road, the A2, to enter Chatham High Street, passing Rochester Railway Station on your left. A short way along the High Street is the ornate building that is still known as the Theatre Royal, though it has not operated as a theatre since 1955.

The Theatre Royal bills itself as the most haunted theatre in England, and with good reason. There are thought to be up to six phantoms in this one building alone. The ghost encountered most often is known, affectionately, as Humphrey. He is dressed smartly in a day suit from the 1920s and is seen most often in the dress circle or the gods above it. In the days when the theatre was staging shows, Humphrey seemed to like watching rehearsals, but these days he may appear at any time. It is thought that he was an assistant manager who worked here in the 1920s and who, one day, failed to turn up for work. He seems to have cleared his rented room and left Chatham in a great hurry, only for his spectre to return a few weeks later.

One of the boxes overlooking the stage is the home of the Green Man. This phantom is dressed all in green: Green suit, green tie, green shirt and presumably, if they could be seen, green shoes. He used to appear when the box was empty for a show, but has not appeared since the theatre closed. Rather more persistent is the elderly lady who has been seen on the ground floor. She appears from time to time, standing quite still and ignoring what goes on around her.

More of a nuisance is the spectral young girl who frequents what used to be the ladies toilets, and are now the toilets for one of the shops that occupy the front of the building. The girl delights in unwinding the rolls of toilet paper, throwing the soap on the floor and such other annoying little habits. A policeman was in the shop one day in the early 1990s when a loud crash sounded from the wash room. The man raced in to find the cubicle door slamming to and fro without any human hands moving it.

The final two ghosts of this much haunted theatre may be one and the same. Charlie Monks, a former member of the front of house staff has put in infrequent appearances in what was once his office, and nearby rooms occasionally reek of a sweet pipe tobacco, although nobody has been smoking. Perhaps they are two distinct entities, but it may be that Charlie Monks has sneaked back for a quiet smoke.

After it closed, the Theatre Royal was converted into shops, with the main auditorium becoming a warehouse. A long running campaign to raise enough funds to restore the Theatre Royal to its former grandeur accepted defeat in 2003 and now a new use is being sought for this grand building.

A little further along the High Street is No. 122. This is a shop which, like so many others, has changed hands and business several times in recent years.

In the 1970s this shop was a clothes shop for young women named Snob. It sold all the latest glam rock fashions to the bright young things of Chatham. Near the front of the premises would be seen from time to time a young woman wearing a sober tweed suit quite out of keeping with the bright gold lamés, gaily printed floral shirts and tinselled jackets that the shop sold. For this reason she stood out and attracted attention. If a shop assistant approached, the girl would push her fingers through her long dark hair, then vanish abruptly. Nobody has reported seeing her recently, but in these more sensible days her tweeds may not seem so incongruous as back in the days of 1970s peacock fashions.

Nearby is a bingo hall that was once a cinema. Staff here have frequently come across a man dressed in an old-style commissionaire's uniform of the type that cinema staff wore in years gone by. He is a resplendent figure in dark green with yellow braid across his chest and on his shoulders. He has been identified as the phantom of William Malan who worked here as the commissionaire for some 20 years from 1929. His task was to greet customers, guide them to their seats and keep mischievous boys in line with his imposing bulk. Despite this, Malan liked children and always said that Saturday matinees were his favourite shows.

Then came the Second World War and Chatham, with its extensive naval dockyards, was a favourite target for the German bombers. Many homes were hit and those homeless families without relatives to stay with were housed temporarily in this cinema. One night a bomber dropped its lethal load on the town centre, badly damaging the cinema. Air raid wardens and others raced to the rescue, and it was Malan who found the bodies of three young children killed in the raid. It is said that Malan never got over the shock.

Perhaps that is why he returns to his old place of work, dressed finely in his smart green uniform. Or perhaps he simply wants to recreate his happy years at work.

5) At the eastern end of Chatham High Street, bear left into Medway Street. At the end of this road, turn left at a T-junction, then left again to join the A231 Dock Road. About 500 yards along this road, turn left into Main Gate Road which leads to the Historic Dockyards.

The first phantom to be found here lurks outside the gates. This particular ghost is never seen, only heard. Late at night, when traffic is silent and peace descends over

The Main Gate to Chatham's historic dockyard is the scene of a nocturnal haunting.

the area, sentries on duty would report hearing footsteps approaching up the road to the main gates. No ordinary footsteps these, but those of a badly limping man who uses a wooden walking stick every other step. The rhythmic tap-tap-tapping would approach the gates, then suddenly cease when the invisible limping man was some 10 feet distant. These days the dockyards are a tourist attraction, not an active naval base, and there are no sentries on duty late at night to hear the ghost. If he still walks.

Within the old dockyards are other phantoms. The most famous of these is none other than Lord Admiral Horatio Nelson, killed in distant waters at the Battle of Trafalgar in 1805. Nelson was born a vicar's son in Norfolk, but joined the navy at the age of 12 as the servant to his uncle, a captain. He worked his way up through the ranks through skill as a seaman and a quick eye for military advantage in a fight. Nelson was a captain at the age of 21 and an admiral at 39. Nelson fought in battles too numerous to mention, losing the sight of his right eye in 1794 and his right arm three years later. Nelson's career climaxed on 21 October 1805 when his fleet met the combined war fleets of Spain and France off Cape Trafalgar, southern Spain. The enemy fleet was annihilated and British control of the

Lord Horatio Nelson, whose phantom has been seen around the Historic Dockyards of Chatham.

high seas was confirmed for more than a century. Nelson was shot down in the moment of victory, his body being brought back to Britain for a state funeral at St Paul's, London.

Soon afterwards, Nelson's ghost began to walk in the dockyards of Chatham. Strangely the phantom does not appear as Nelson did when he died, but as a young man complete with both arms and both eyes. He strides purposefully past the Commissioners' House and down to the naval docks themselves.

The Commissioners' House, a grand 18th century house, is haunted by three ghosts. The first lurks in the attic, an area closed to visitors. She is of a little old lady dressed all in black. It is thought she might be a housekeeper from days long gone, for she is most active around the linen cupboard. The other ghosts are a pair of gentlemen who stand on the back lawn of the house in furious argument. Judged by their dress, these men date to the earlier days of Chatham's naval history around 1680. The cause of their dispute is unknown for, despite the fact that they are shouting angrily at each other, their voices cannot be heard.

6) It is possible to return to Rochester Castle by retracing your steps, or you can take one of the pleasure boats that ply between the Historic Dockyards and Rochester Bridge.

Ships of war from the time of Nelson.

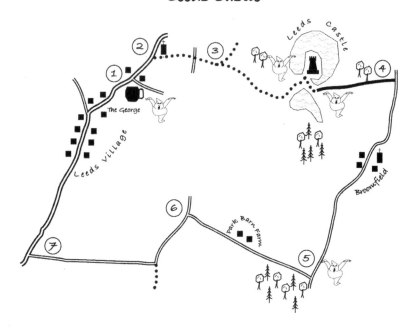

Walk No.4
Leeds Castle

The monks that flit about Leeds village are quiet and distinctly non-frightening ghosts.

Leeds Castle

Distance:	**4 miles**
Ghostly Rating:	*** * ***
Route:	**Leeds - Broomfield - Leeds**
Map:	**OS Explorer 148**
Start/Parking:	**In Leeds Village, near the George Pub.**
Public Transport:	**The bus route No.12 runs from Maidstone Hospital to Leeds and on to Tenterden.**
Conditions:	**This route is largely over well-maintained lanes and bridlepaths.**
Refreshments:	**There are two pubs in Leeds together with a shop which sells soft drinks and snacks.**

This is a gentle walk that takes in what must be the most scenically beautiful castle in England. The walk passes beneath the walls of the castle, as well as taking in the adjacent villages and exploring part of the valley of the River Len. The ghosts to be found here speak of the castle's past, and of a now vanished structure that once dominated the upper Len Valley.

The Walk

1) Park in the high street of the village of Leeds, close to The George public house. The lane running beside the pub is George Lane.

Although there is nothing to show above ground today, this lane and the fields south of it was for some centuries the site of the Augustinian Priory from which the Abbey Farm takes its name. Excavations in the 1970s have shown that the buildings were extensive and reached beyond the field into the woods behind. The Priory was founded in 1119 and dedicated to St Mary and St Nicholas. As with many other medieval religious houses, Leeds Priory was closed down by King Henry VIII during the Reformation, in 1539, and converted into a comfortable mansion for the local gentry. This house was demolished in the 1780s after it fell

A tomb from the churchyard at Leeds.

The church at Leeds.

into disrepair, though one wall remained standing until the early 20th century.

Perhaps inevitably there has been talk about ghostly monks flitting around this field and the nearby woods. Although the stories are common, actual witnesses are rare so it is not entirely certain if this is a true haunting or just a dim memory of the days when monks really did walk the streets of Leeds.

2) Continue north along the High Street. Turn right at the church, following the footpath that runs through the churchyard to the right of the church. Exit the churchyard by a kissing gate and continue along the path across an open grass field.

3) Where this path meets a lane, cross straight over through another kissing gate and continue alongside the left side of the field. Cross into a second field. At the far side of this field enter the grounds of Leeds Castle. Ignore the path bearing off to the left, but continue straight on around the shoulder of a hill until Leeds Castle comes into view.

This beautiful castle is an ancient one. It takes its name from an English nobleman named Leedian who built a manor here in the 9th century. Although no trace of Leedian's home remains, it would probably have been a grand wooden hall with stables and other outbuildings. Not until the Normans came was a castle built here. That early castle was bought in 1278 by

The path enters the grounds of Leeds Castle by way of a kissing gate.

Eleanor of Castile, queen to King Edward I, who began the buildings that are seen today, with some extensive modernisation being carried out in Victorian times.

There are said to be two ghosts here. The first is a gentle and anonymous lady. Dressed in a pale dress and brushing her long, dark hair she is seen in the grounds of the castle.

The second phantom is altogether more dangerous. This is the ghost of a Duchess of Gloucester who was imprisoned here from 1450 onwards. She had been married to Humphrey, Duke of Gloucester, who earned the nickname "Good Duke Humphrey" for the efficient and honest way in which he ran the government of England for his brother, King Henry V, while the latter was busy fighting wars in France. After Humphrey's death in 1447, his widow seems to have become slightly deranged. She indulged in both heresy and witchcraft at a time when both the Church and ordinary folk condemned such things. She was arrested in 1450 but, being the aunt of the then King Henry VI, avoided execution. Instead she was sent to Leeds Castle to face perpetual imprisonment. The castle provided security for those outside, and comfort for the Duchess inside. Inevitably she became known as the Wicked Duchess in contrast to her husband, the Good Duke.

Long after her death the dark-robed ghost of the half mad Wicked Duchess would stalk the corridors of Leeds Castle. She has not been seen for many years, which is probably just as well, but she is closely linked to a phantom that is still very active and which will be met later on this walk.

4) Continue down the hill and turn right in front of the castle to cross the causeway between the two lakes. Beyond the causeway, turn left to pass in front of the outbuildings and follow a drive towards a pair of gatehouses. Beyond the gateway the drive opens on to a lane. Turn right.

Leeds Castle is famously one of the most beautiful in England.

5) Follow this lane downhill to cross the River Len, then continue up the far side of the valley. As the lane enters the small village of Broomfield it passes the church on the left. The lane continues uphill beyond the village. Take the first right to walk past Park Barn Farm to a T-junction.

These lanes are the haunt of a most dangerous phantom: The Black Dog of Leeds. This is no ordinary dog, even for a ghost. It is a gigantic beast, standing as tall as a man with muscular, thickset body and legs rippling with muscles. Its eyes are unnaturally round and wide, glowing with a deep malevolent fire of flame red. The dog patrols these lanes, searching for lone walkers and travellers. If this beast passes you by without a glance you may count yourself lucky, for its glance brings bad luck and even death.

Local legend has it that this is the Devil's hound, conjured up from Hell by the Wicked Duchess. It is said that while she sat imprisoned in the castle, the Wicked Duchess sent out this hound from hell to work her evil for her. She sent it to kill, to maim and to cast spells. Although the Duchess has long gone to whatever fate awaited her, the Black Dog remains. It is best to avoid it, if you get the chance.

6) At the T-junction turn left, then follow the lane to the right walking downhill across open fields that give good views to both north and south.

7) At another T-junction turn right, walking downhill along this lane to return to Leeds village.

The gatehouses that guard the rear or southern entrance to Leeds Castle estate.

The quiet lane that returns to Leeds village from Leeds Castle.

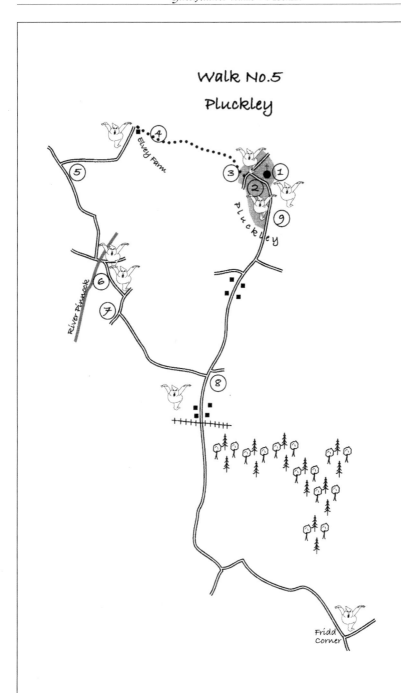

Walk No.5
Pluckley

Pluckley

Distance:	**5 miles (8 miles with optional excursion)**
Ghostly Rating:	*** * * * * * * * * * * ***
Route:	**Pluckley - Chambers' Green - Pluckley**
Map:	**OS Explorer 137**
Start/Parking:	**In Pluckley village centre, near the church**
Public Transport:	**The walk can be accessed from Pluckley Railway Station at Point 8.**
Conditions:	**A walk that covers generally level terrain with just a few short hills. Most of the route is over surfaced tracks and lanes, with one cross-country section that can be muddy after rain.**
Refreshments:	**The walk passes one pub in Pluckley and a second at Chambers' Green. The little shop opposite the church in Pluckley offers drinks, sweets, crisps and the like.**

Pluckley is without doubt the most haunted village in Kent, and its residents will tell you it is the most haunted in England. There are certainly ghosts in plenty here, and some are quite spectacular. The most dramatic haunting lies a mile or more south of the main walk, and a two-way excursion is added to this walk for those who feel energetic enough to make it.

The Walk

1) Park in the High Street near the church.

The first ghost to be encountered is in the churchyard. This is the Red Lady Dering, one of the more active ghosts in this village. She seems to be searching the churchyard for one gravestone in particular, but it is a gravestone she will never find. The ghost is that of a Lady Dering from the 17th century. She died in childbirth, as did the baby to which she was

The village sign to Pluckley, perhaps the most haunted village in England.

Pluckley Church, scene of more than one haunting.

giving birth. Lady Dering herself was properly buried as befitted the lady of the manor, but the baby has no headstone to mark its grave. It died before it could be baptised and although buried in consecrated land it had no tomb. It is presumed that it is for the grave of her beloved baby that the sad Red Lady Dering searches so diligently.

Inside the church is to be found the Dering Chapel, a small space set aside for worship by this local family and for the burial of their dead. One of the Lady Dering's interred here was buried inside three lead coffins, each placed within the next. It was said that this was because her husband knew her to be a wicked woman and was determined that her burial should be final. If this were so, it is not clear why the grieving widower should lay a single red rose on the lady's breast just as the first coffin was closed. Whatever the truth, the spirit of this Lady Dering, carrying her single red rose, has not rested quietly. She has been seen several times kneeling in the Dering Chapel as if in prayer. Perhaps to seek forgiveness for her wickedness, whatever it was.

There are stories of a second ghost being seen inside the church. This is of a woman in fairly modern dress, that of the 1970s. She is seen entering the church as if on a casual visit, but promptly vanishes and is never seen to leave. There is also said to be a white dog, but firm accounts of this spectral hound are elusive.

2) Leave the churchyard and turn right, walking northwest to the Black Horse pub on your right.

The High Street, in which the pub stands, is haunted by the sounds of a passing horse-drawn carriage. In recent years, only the sound of hooves on the road and the clattering of wheels has been heard, but in years gone by the spectral vehicle was seen as well. Old accounts have it that the vehicle is a grand carriage driven by a

The haunted Black Horse public house stands in the heart of Pluckley.

The path down to Elvey Farm Hotel runs across open countryside.

coachman perched on a high seat, and carrying shadowy figures in a gloomy interior.

The Black Horse itself is also haunted, again by an invisible phantom. This ghost is not only never seen, but is not heard either. He makes himself known by moving furniture around, hiding small objects and generally being a bit of a nuisance. For some reason the phantom has a particular penchant for moving coats. A coat may be hung over the back of a chair, but will mysteriously make its way to the hook by the door. It is presumed that the ghost is that of a former landlord keen to tidy up his pub, but nobody is really certain.

3) At the T-junction turn left down the hill, then right along a driveway signposted as the Greensand Way. At the end of the lane pass through a gate into a field which can be marshy in wet weather. At the far side of the field pass through another gate, then a third almost immediately. This gives access to a wide sloping field with a gate visible on the far side. Pass through this gate to enter a large field with no obvious exit. Walk across the field in the direction indicated by the signpost by the gate to find a small gate tucked away in a patch of brambles.

4) Pass through this gate and turn sharp right to walk along the field edge to a gate visible on the edge of a clump of trees. Pass through this gate and then across a smaller field to enter the narrow drive that gives access to Elvey Farm, now a comfortable country house hotel.

This farm plays host to a rather harmless, sad spectre. He is the ghost of a young man, aged in his twenties, with blond hair and a thin, wispy beard. He was the farmer here in the early 19th century who shot himself in the dairy a few days after his beautiful young wife had died of a fever. The poor young man causes no trouble and is not even especially frightening. He is so solid and natural looking that people mistake him for a visitor. For some unexplained reason the distinctive odour of singed wool is smelled when he appears.

5) Continue along the drive to reach a lane at a T-junction. Turn left. Follow this lane to a second T-Junction. Turn left to cross the narrow, overgrown Pinnock Stream.

The stream is today carried under the road by a culvert, but in days gone by this was a ford beside which was a small wooden footbridge. An old lady habitually sat here selling the watercress that she grew in the Pinnock by her cottage, a short distance downstream. Exactly what happened to her one gruesome day is unclear, for nobody was around at the time to see. A passerby found her badly burned and charred body slumped beside the bridge, almost totally consumed by fire. At the time it was thought that she must have fallen asleep and her clay pipe somehow set her clothes on fire.

Soon afterwards, however, the old lady's ghost began to be seen. She appeared consumed by flames that leapt up from all around her in a dramatic show of blazing yellow light. Some whispered she must have been murdered by someone who covered her with oil or pitch before setting her alight. More recently it has been suggested that she was a victim of what is now termed spontaneous human combustion – a rare event for which there is no adequate scientific explanation.

Whatever really happened here all those years ago the ghost is fading from sight. Witnesses are no longer forced to endure the gruesome sight of an old lady burning to death. Instead there is merely a bright light that soon subsides to a red glow, as if of an ember in a grate.

6) Just beyond the stream turn right.

On the right a hundred yards or more along this lane is Rose Farm. Many years ago the lady who lived here ate some berries she had gathered in nearby fields, and promptly died. It was assumed she had mistakenly picked some poisonous berries, though quite how a country woman made such a mistake is unclear. Her ghost has been seen around the farm from time to time, but she causes no nuisance to anyone.

The little Pinnock Stream is the focus of a startling haunting, though it is little seen these days.

7) At the end of the lane is a T-junction. Turn right, then quickly left. This lane runs down to reach a T-junction at Chambers' Green. Turn right towards the station.

On the right is the entrance to what is now a small industrial estate, but in years gone by was a pit from which clay was extracted for turning into bricks. The air here can be torn asunder by an ear-splitting scream - the phantom voice of a worker who met a grisly end in the claypit some years ago when he fell and tumbled down the sheer walls to his death.

8) To take the optional excursion to Fridd Corner, cross the railway bridge and, just before Stanford Bridge Farm, a footpath is signposted to the left. This path will cross fields and woodland to emerge eventually on a lane just north of Fridd Corner. It is, however, very overgrown and tough going. An easier option is to continue past the farm to cross a stream. The lane bends left then sharp right. Bear left here on to a very narrow and quiet lane which winds across fields to reach a T-junction at Fridd Corner itself. Return to Chambers' Green the way you have come.

Fridd Corner, south of the village, where many passers-by have been frightened by ghosts.

The ghost at Fridd Corner more than repays the effort of getting here - although it traditionally appears only on moonlit nights. There is not just one ghost here, but a whole crowd of them. Some two centuries ago a highwayman was pursued by a group of irate would-be victims after a robbery went wrong. The highwayman's horse stumbled as he rounded this corner and the man was thrown to the ground.

Scrambling to his feet, the highwayman backed against one of the trees here to fight for his life. Using pistols and sword he held off his pursuers for some time. Eventually they overwhelmed him and a sword pinned the man to the tree trunk behind him. There his body was left to hang while life gradually bled away. His killers did not move the body until morning, when they brought a cart to take it away for burial.

The entire fight from start to finish is played out in spectral form from time to time. More usually, however, the dead body of the highwayman is seen pinned to a tree. More than one passing motorist has hurriedly informed the police of the corpse, but it is only the phantom.

9) If not taking the excursion to Fridd Corner, turn around and walk north along Station Road, away from Chambers' Green. Follow this lane back into Pluckley. As you climb into the village, the lane turns sharp left where a pair of fine gates stand on the right.

These gates once gave access to Dering House, though now they remain firmly locked and behind them is only an overgrown track through woods. In the days when the Dering Family were squires in these parts, their mansion stood at the end of the lane, but it burned down in the 1950s. By that time the Derings had long since left Pluckley and their old home was housing a boys' school. The house and grounds were haunted by a grey lady, apparently yet another phantom Lady Dering. On one occasion in the 1930s, a schoolmaster who saw the ghost was convinced that it was a realistic prank got up by the boys. He whipped an old army pistol from his desk and fired over the phantom's head and shouted loudly for the boys to own up. None did and the ghost abruptly vanished.

Continue past the gates. As you approach the church you will see the old Victorian school on the left.

The old school at Pluckley plays host to a ghostly schoolmaster in frock coat.

This stretch of road is haunted by the ghost of the early Victorian schoolmaster who killed himself here. The reasons for the suicide never came to light. The man had only recently been appointed to the village school and nobody in Pluckley knew of any troubles that affected him. Before taking his life, the distraught man had dressed himself in his finest frock coat and striped trousers. It is in this outfit that his ghost appears as it strides purposefully towards the school from the side turning known as Dicky Buss Lane.

Pluckley certainly lives up to its reputation as being a most haunted little village.

Walk No.6
Penshurst

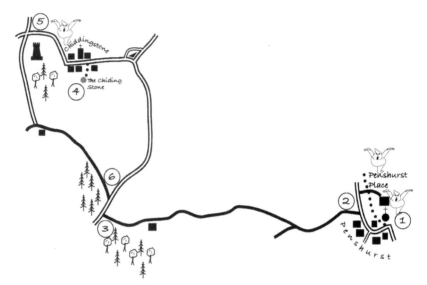

The walk begins in the churchyard at Penshurst.

Penshurst

Distance:	**6 miles**
Ghostly Rating:	**＊＊＊＊**
Route:	**Penshurst - Chiddingstone - Penshurst**
Map:	**OS Explorer 147**
Start/Parking:	**Penshurst village**
Conditions:	**This walk covers both village centres, where the going is over paths and lanes, linked by a bridleway which is well surfaced, but can be slippery in very wet weather.**
Refreshments:	**There is a pub in Penshurst and another in Chiddingstone, both offering meals. Penshurst Place offers a small cafe.**

This walk links two of the more charming villages in Kent, both of which are dominated by historic houses. The families that once lived in these grand houses were, of course, friendly with each other. That friendship has left its phantom mark on this walk for the relationship between the two led to one of the hauntings that make this a more than usually spinechilling ramble.

The Walk

1) Park in Penshurst and make your way to the churchyard. From the churchyard a gateway gives access to the gardens of the old vicarage.

The Vicarage is a handsome house built in the reign of Queen Anne in local red brick. It is a private house, but the gateway leading to it is haunted by a young man dressed in the smock and rough work clothes that were the habitual dress of farm labourers for generations. The ghost walks up the path from the village with determined stride, turning in at the gate but vanishing before he reaches the front door. He is said to be a local farmboy who fell in love with the daughter of the vicar back in the late 18th century. The girl returned his feelings, but the vicar had rather higher hopes for the matrimonial prospects of his daughter than a penniless labourer, no matter how handsome he might have been.

The haunted gate in the churchyard at Penshurst leads to the elegant old rectory, now a private house.

The beautiful mansion of Penshurst Place dominates the village of the same name.

Contrary to the course of most such clandestine love affairs, this one ended happily. The farmboy eventually persuaded the vicar of his honest intentions and his capacity for hard work. The marriage went ahead. Perhaps the ghostly lover recreates the journey he took to persuade his future father-in-law of his merits. He certainly has a determined enough stride.

Continue along the path through the churchyard, passing over a narrow stile and emerging into a wide open field. Behind the hedge to your right is Penshurst Place.

Penshurst is, however, best known for the stately pile of Penshurst Place which stands at the eastern edge of the village. The heart of the house is the Great Hall, built in the 14th century for the wealthy merchant Sir John de Pulteney, who was elected Lord Mayor of London no less than four times in the 1330s. The house was greatly extended and the gardens laid out in the 16th century after the property came into the possession of the Sidney family.

The enigmatic female ghost that lurks in the gardens is thought to be an early member of the Sidney family. She wears a ruff around her neck, a typical fashion of later Tudor times, and seems to take a great interest in the area of the gardens that were laid out at that period. A very similar phantom has been seen, though only rarely, walking up the main staircase. It may be the same ghost, or may be somebody quite different.

By far the most famous ghost to be met on this walk, however, is the impressive gentleman who has been seen around Penshurst Place dressed in colourful doublet and hose. This is Sir Philip Sidney, who was born here on 30 November 1554. At the age of just 18, Philip had the misfortune to be in Paris on the feast day of St Bartholomew, the day on which the Catholics had secretly fixed for an uprising and massacre of the French Protestants. Thousands were slaughtered in a series of murders, riots and street fights. Young Philip fled to the home of the English ambassador, Sir Francis Walsingham, where they barricaded themselves in.

In 1575 Philip was introduced at court and quickly found favour with Queen Elizabeth I through his good looks, ready wit and elegant poetry. Soon afterwards he married the daughter of his old friend Walsingham, now head of the secret service, and was knighted.

His reputation as a poet and writer grew as quickly as did his fame as a soldier. Sir Philip rose through the ranks of courtiers and worked his way up through state appointments until, in 1585, he was made Master of the Ordnance.

It was occupying this office which brought him to Zutphen the following year. The Dutch were in the midst of a war through which they would free themselves from Spanish rule. On 22 September a Spanish army attacked Zutphen, and Sidney volunteered to lead the local cavalry militia. In the course of a gallant and successful charge he was badly wounded in the leg. Carried back to Zutphen, Sidney was given a flask of water, but passed it to a dying man declaring "Your need is greater than my own". Sadly, Sidney's wound became infected and he died a month later. His body was brought back to England and buried in St Paul's Cathedral, London.

His ghost has been seen walking around Penshurst Place and its grounds where his descendants still live. It has not, however, been seen in recent years.

2) Continue across the field to meet the drive to Penshurst Place. Turn left down the drive to meet a lane. Turn left at the lane. Follow the lane for about 200 yards, then turn right into a driveway. This drive forms part of the Eden Valley Walk. Where the drive forks, bear right continuing along the Eden Valley Walk.

3) This route eventually emerges on to a lane. Turn right. Follow this lane across open fields. Where an oddly-shaped house stands in the angle of a road junction, turn left. This lane runs into Chiddingstone. As you enter the village a small green with a bench stands on the left. A footpath across the green gives access to the ancient Chiding Stone.

The massive block of sandstone is the Chiding Stone that gives Chiddingstone its name. The stone has attracted many rumours, stories and legends which attempt to explain its presence, but it has never been properly studied by archaeologists. It is generally thought to be a natural spur that was carved to shape for mysterious religious reasons during the Bronze Age, over three

The enigmatic Chiding Stone around which swirl many stories.

thousand years ago. The name is, however, comparatively modern. One story says it derives from Cidda, the Saxon thegn who owned this manor in the 7th century. Alternatively others think the name derives from the fact that local wrongdoers would be dragged here by villagers for a very public chiding, or telling off, accompanied by such a thrashing as the locals deemed necessary. Or again the stone may have been a sacrificial stone used by the druids; or a stone marker linked to the pagan religion of the early English.

Where the lane divides north of Chiddingstone Castle, the route of the walk bears to the left.

The route back to Penshurst follows part of the Eden Valley Walk, which is well signposted.

Perhaps one day a proper scientific study may reveal the truth.

4) Returning to the lane, turn left and continue into the village. Follow the lane as it bends sharp right, with the back gates to Chiddingstone Castle straight in front of you. After crossing a dammed stream the lane bends left.

The ghost of Chiddingstone may be encountered in any of these lanes near the castle. She is an attractive young lady mounted on a prancing bay horse which trots swiftly along. This dark-haired girl wears a tricorn hat and a tightly-fitting jacket of a dark colour, perhaps a dark green if one witness is to be believed. Local rumour has it that she is Anne, a daughter of the Sidneys of Penshurst Place, who married into the Streatfield family of Chiddingstone Castle. This would date her to the early 17th century. This lady is said to have lived to a great age and, soon after she died, to have returned as a phantom of herself as a young lady to ride the lanes around Chiddingstone Castle.

5) At the cross roads, turn left. Follow this lane to a turning on the left that appears to be the driveway to a private house. This is, in fact, a continuation of the Eden Valley Walk. Follow the clear signage for the Walk past the houses and across fields into a wood.

6) At the far end of the wood, the path meets a lane. Turn right. After just 100 yards, turn left. This is the section of the Eden Valley Walk that you followed on your way out. Follow the Walk back to Penshurst.

The Eden Valley Walk crosses an open field before joining a surfaced byway.

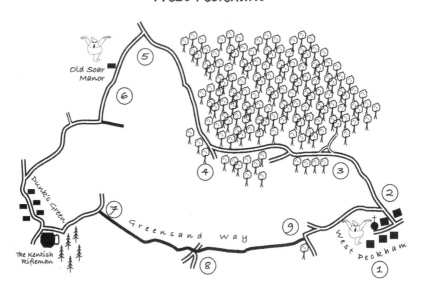

Walk No.7
West Peckham

Old Soar Manor

Dunk's Green

The Kentish Rifleman

Greensand Way

West Peckham

The village green at West Peckham is flanked by the two staples of English village life: church and pub.

West Peckham

Distance:	**6 miles**
Ghostly Rating:	******
Route:	**West Peckham - Old Soar - Dunk's Green - West Peckham**
Map:	**OS Explorer 148**
Start/Parking:	**West Peckham.**
Conditions:	**This route is largely over well-maintained lanes or byways, though one section of footpath can be boggy in wet weather.**
Refreshments:	**There is a pub at West Peckham and another at Dunk's Green, both of which offer meals.**

There are some steepish hills on this walk, but nothing too strenuous and the effort is rewarded by some fine views. Most of the route is over good surfaces and the walking is fairly easy. The two ghosts to be encountered on this walk are very different – one a notorious crook and the other a gentle young woman. But mystery surrounds them both and neither is quite what they at first seem.

The Walk

1) Park in West Peckham and find the church. From the church walk east to find a lane turning left signposted to Plaxtol. Turn left.

West Peckham was once the home of a notorious criminal who went by the name of Jack Diamond. This was not, of course, his real name but was the nickname he acquired through his habit of wearing diamond cufflinks and rings.

Jack was already middle aged when he moved here in the later 18th century. He bought a little cottage in the village and announced that he had found the rural retreat to which he wished to retire after a long and arduous career as a merchant in London. Of course, he said, he would need to return to the city from time to time, but mostly he intended to be a gentleman of leisure. And, to all appearances, that is what Jack Diamond became. He spent his days walking around the village and nearby lanes, passed time in the local inns without overindulgence and became a regular worshipper at the little church with its ancient peel of bells.

Every now and then Jack Diamond would leave for a few days, saying he was heading for London to attend to some business. Then he would return to resume his blameless and quiet life.

The route north of West Peckham has been designated a Quiet Lane by the Council.

But one terrible morning a violent storm swept down over Kent and to West Peckham in particular. It was a Friday 13th and early in the morning when the storm struck. At 6.30am a ferocious bolt of lightning crashed down from the angry skies to hit West Peckham with a terrifying jolt. Jack Diamond's cottage took the full force of the blast. Jack himself was killed instantly and the building damaged beyond repair.

Neighbours rushed to the ruins, and were amazed by what they found. Jack Diamond's cottage was stuffed full of expensive items – jewellery, watches, silver tableware and valuables of all kinds. Amazement slowly turned to horror as it emerged over the following days that the items were stolen. The idea quickly took hold that Diamond had been a highwayman, burglar and thief – perhaps much worse. The stolen items were returned to their rightful owners, Diamond given a decent burial and the scandal slowly faded into history.

Until, that is, another Friday 13th came around. Farm workers up early that morning clearly saw Jack Diamond walking down the lane to his vanished cottage in West Peckham. And on the stroke of 6.30am a terrified and terrifying scream tore through the air of the village. So it has continued every Friday 13th since. The ghost of a middle aged man is seen walking towards the village, then a scream is heard.

It seems Jack Diamond has not left West Peckham at all.

2) Walk up Forge Lane until it bends left. Go straight on up Stans Lane, signposted as a "quiet Lane".

3) At the top of the hill the lane enters dense, coppiced woodland. Where the road forks, go left, then after just a short distance turn left at a crossroads. Where the lane forks in the midst of the woodlands, bear right.

4) At the end of the lane is a T-junction. Turn right to continue through the woodland for a distance before emerging onto open farmland.

5) Turn left down a short, steep hill. This lane leads down into a wooded hollow where stands Old Soar Manor.

This magnificent medieval manor house is now in the care of the National Trust, and is open to the public most of the year. The heart of the building is 13th century and includes the rare survival of the lord's private apartments and chapel. In most halls and manors, these fairly rudimentary chambers have long since been replaced by more genteel rooms for the convenience of the owner. At Old Soar, however, the new rooms were simply added on the side and the older rooms left in their original condition.

The haunting here is rather disturbing. It dates back to the year 1775 when the then owners, the Catholic Geary family, were preparing to celebrate Christmas. They had brought a Catholic priest over from the continent to help with the religious side of the festivities and he was occupying a room in the older part of the house while preparing the medieval chapel for the big day. Among the domestic staff working in the kitchens was a scullery maid named Jenny, who was walking out with a local farm worker whom she planned to marry the next year.

Late on Christmas Eve, Jenny was returning to her room after finishing a task in the kitchens when she ran into the priest. The priest, who was drunk, dragged Jenny into the chapel and raped her. Poor Jenny was terrified. She did not think anyone would believe her and, simple country girl that she was, was deeply shocked that a priest could behave in such a manner. Before long Jenny's predicament got far worse. She was pregnant.

At first she went to her boyfriend with her story, but he refused to believe her. He threw her out of his home,

The walk passes through extensive stands of coppiced chestnut trees.

declaring that she was a wanton who had made up the story to cover her licentious behaviour. So Jenny went to see the priest, who was still at Old Soar. She found him in the chapel. Three hours later her cold, lifeless body was found in that holy place. Her skull was smashed in, the girl having apparently fallen against the sharp edge of the stone piscina near the altar.

The old and the new. There is no mistaking the route to the haunted Old Soar Manor.

The priest later reported that the girl had come to him to seek spiritual guidance in her awkward and delicate condition. He, of course, denied the story of rape and instead claimed that she had told him the father was the heartless farm worker who had thrown her out. The priest said he had advised her to seek the grace of God in prayer, then try again to talk to her estranged boyfriend. Then, he said, he had left her. The accident that caused her death must have happened some time after that.

The priest was believed, he was after all a priest. Jenny was buried at Plaxtol Church though a few thought she may have committed suicide and should therefore be banned from sacred ground. A few days later it came time for the priest to leave, so he travelled to Dover and took ship to France.

It was after he was gone that the hauntings began. Lights were seen in the chapel when

The windows of Old Soar Manor have been known to shine with a phantom light that is not of this world.

the room was empty and footsteps echoed around the room when nobody was moving. As time passed the hauntings became more pronounced, rather than fading away. Eventually the phantom of Jenny herself was seen. Sometimes she was seen in the chapel, but sometimes strolling gently around the grounds of the manor.

But this was a ghost with a message. On rare occasions the phantom acted out the last moments of poor Jenny's life. Those who saw the apparition were left in no doubt that it had been no accident. Though Jenny's was the only ghost to be seen it was clear that she was struggling desperately against some unseen attacker. Whoever it was assaulting Jenny slammed her head repeatedly against the piscina, until the still body of the girl slumped to the floor, then vanished.

Unfortunately the priest was by this time long gone and beyond the arm of English justice. It is to be hoped that divine judgement proved more effective.

The more disturbing aspects of the haunting seem to have faded over the years. These days Jenny is most likely to be seen strolling gently through the gardens or standing quietly in the chapel. Perhaps she is now able to relive happier days.

6) Leaving Old Soar Manor, turn right along the lane. Ignore a byway to the left and a lane to the right and follow the lane to a T-junction. Turn left into the village of Dunk's Green, turning left in front of the Kentish Rifleman pub.

7) Where this lane bends sharp left, turn right along a footpath signposted as part of the Greensand Way. This clearly signposted route cuts diagonally across an orchard, then across open land to pass a large pond on the right and a wood on the left. It then runs alongside a house and garden to emerge on to a lane.

8) Cross the lane to rejoin the footpath signed as the Greensand Way. This path becomes a broad track before emerging on to a lane.

9) Turn left then quickly right at a T-junction and follow this lane back into West Peckham.

The older men of the Home Guard who protected Kent during World War II are commemorated on a pub sign in Dunk's Green.

Where the path crosses a lane, it climbs out by way of these uneven steps.

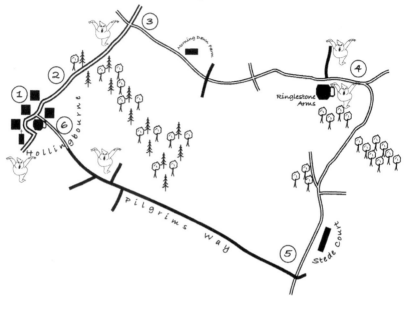

Walk No.8
Hollingbourne

A horseman in 18th century clothing has been seen riding up the High Street of Hollingbourne.

Hollingbourne

Distance:	7 miles
Ghostly Rating:	*****
Route:	Hollingbourne - Ringlestone - Hollingbourne
Map:	OS Explorer 148
Start/Parking:	Hollingbourne, close to the church.
Public Transport:	Hollingbourne is on the railway, though it is almost a mile from the station to the village.
Conditions:	This route is largely over quiet country lanes, with one lengthy stretch over a public byway.
Refreshments:	The haunted pub at Ringlestone offers good meals.

This is a hilly outing taking the walker over the rolling North Downs and dipping down into the valley of the Snagbrook. In places the hills can be steep, but they are not too demanding as the steepest sections are on country lanes where the tarmac surface makes for easy walking. The route offers magnificent views south over central Kent and west to Maidstone as well as some unusual and idiosyncratic phantoms.

The Walk

1) Park in Hollingbourne and make your way to the church.

Back in the mid-17th century Lady Grace Gethin was a noted young beauty among the local gentry in this part of Kent. Her devotion to God was as notable as her good looks and she regularly attended worship here at her parish church. One Sunday young Lady Grace suddenly leapt to her feet in the middle of the service, gave a strangled cry and collapsed in a faint. Anxious relatives and villagers clustered round, but it was some time before she regained her senses. When she did, Lady Grace explained that she had witnessed a vision so remarkable that the good folk of Hollingbourne carved the poor

The lychgate into the churchyard of Hollingbourne near which a ghostly lady materialises before striding towards the church.

The lane from Hollingbourne to Ringlestone is narrow and quiet.

girl a beautiful tomb, inscribed with the story and set it up in the chancel of the church.

The tablet remains to this day and reads:

"She was vouchsafed in a miraculous manner an immediate prospect of her future blisse for ye space of two houres to ye astonishment of all about her and being like St Paul in an inexpressible transport of joy thereby fully evidencing her foresight of the heavenly glory in inconceivable raptures triumphing over death and continuing sensible to ye last she resigned her pious soul to God and victoriously entered rest."

The next day Lady Grace died secure in the faith that her vision foretold her journey to heaven.

Wherever her soul may have gone, her ghost returns occasionally to Hollingbourne. Her slight figure, wearing a straw bonnet and dressed in the height of fashion for the era when she lived, walks slowly from the lychgate across the churchyard.

2) From the church, follow the main village street northward past the Dirty Habit pub and a crossroads. Continue straight on up a steep hill out of the village.

This hill is haunted by a phantom horseman, who trots along quite sedately as he rides up the hill. This is the phantom of a man named Duppa who lived in Hollingbourne House, at the top of the hill, in the 17th century. This particular ghost appears to be quite normal and solid when he is seen. There are no semi-transparent bodies to give away his spectral nature, nor does he ride in mid-air. He can, however, be recognised by his hat with a broad, floppy brim and by his highly ornate spurs that jingle as he trots along. His ghostly nature becomes startlingly apparent when he reaches the gates of Hollingbourne House, where he vanishes into thin air.

3) Walk up the hill to reach the gates of Hollingbourne House. Just beyond the gates, the lane reaches a crossroads. Turn right. This quiet, narrow lane passes a farm with the quaint name of Morning Dawn, before meeting a crossroads. Go straight ahead and

The Ringlestone Arms has a noisy ghost.

Farm buildings near the top of the hill in Hogbarn Lane.

down a gentle slope to find the Ringlestone Arms Hotel on the right.

This ancient pub is the largest building in the hamlet of Ringlestone. It is haunted by a ghost who puts in his appearance at any time of the day or night at any season of the year. Not that anybody has ever seen this particular ghost, but everyone knows when he is about. Suddenly there will come strange sounds from the cellar. At first it sounds as if a man in heavy boots is stomping about downstairs, then come noises similar to barrels being rolled about. After a while, a short silence follows, after which the footsteps begin again. The ghost heads for the steps that lead up to the ground floor. He stomps up the steps with quite unnecessary vigour. When on the point of reaching the ground floor, the footsteps suddenly cease.

Time and again the performance has been gone through by the ghostly man, but he has never yet actually reached the bar. No doubt this is much to the relief of any customers who may be quenching their thirsts at the time.

The byway running north opposite the pub has an evil reputation. Details are scanty, but more than one person using this route to Wormshill and Frinsted has had the feeling of being watched by something quite malevolent. One witness claimed to see a strange, drifting grey shape, but they did not stay long enough to get a good look.

4) Continue past the Ringlestone Arms Hotel as the lane dips into a valley. Where the lane veers left, turn right up Hogbarn Lane. This climbs steeply and bends right. Ignore a turning to the right, then another to the left and pass Stede Court.

5) The lane then plunges steeply down a hill towards the village of Harrietsham. Almost at the foot of the hill is a crossroads. Turn right into a track signposted as part of the North Downs Way. Beyond Hillside Farm the track becomes a byway which runs along the face of the hill offering views to the south across the valley of the River Len, and the modern M20. After a mile and a half the byway edges to the left of a wood that comes down the hill from

The entrance to the Pilgrims Way just beyond Stede Court.

the right. It then strikes out across open fields once more.

This section of the North Downs Way follows the ancient track known today as the Pilgrims Way. The name derives from the fact that it was used extensively during the medieval period by pilgrims heading for Canterbury to worship at the shrine of St Thomas Becket, but the route is much older than that. Its eastern end rests on the English Channel at Folkestone. It then climbs up to run along the southern face of the North Downs, crossing the Stour and Medway rivers before entering Surrey and heading west to peter out on the heights of Salisbury Plain. The route was old when the Romans came, and may date back as far as 6,000 years or more. By following the high ground the route offered firm footing for early travellers, when valley floors were prone to flood or become boggy after rain.

However old the route is, the phantom Wild Rider who haunts this section is of similarly ancient, but unknown date. He rides towards Hollingbourne with a haste that seems almost suicidal. He whips his horse as he races on at full gallop, ignoring walkers, deep ruts or other obstacles. In his wild-eyed haste to get on he has no time for such things. Strangely the man rides in absolute silence. The hooves of his horse make no sound as they pound the ground, nor are his shouts heard. After dark, it is quite the reverse. The sound of a galloping horse, urged on by a shouting man can be clearly heard, but no phantom is seen.

6) Continue along the North Downs Way until it emerges into the high street of Hollingbourne. Turn left to return to the church.

The stretch of the Pilgrims Way that is haunted by an ancient and startling apparition.

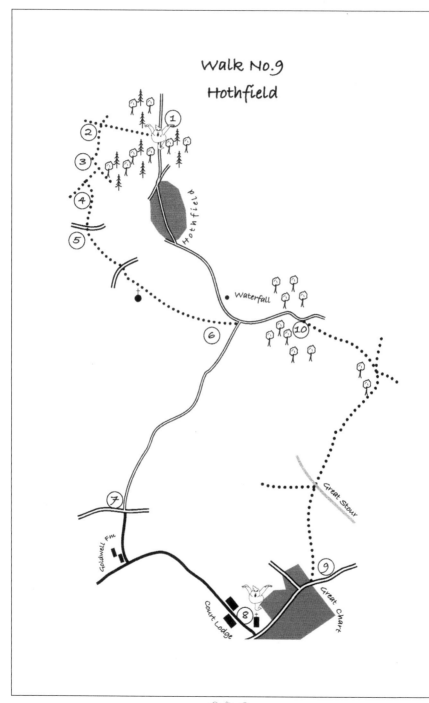

Walk No.9
Hothfield

Hothfield

Distance:	8 miles
Ghostly Rating:	**
Route:	Hothfield Common - Goldwell - Great Chart - Hothfield - Hothfield Common
Map:	OS Explorer 137
Start/Parking:	Hothfield Common Car Park
Public Transport:	Great Chart can be reached by bus from Canterbury. The walk can be joined at Point 9.
Conditions:	A walk that crosses a wide variety of landscape and habitat from bogs and dense woodland to open hillsides. The majority of the route is across unsurfaced paths. The going can be difficult in bad weather, but is generally easy in drier conditions.
Refreshments:	The walk passes a pub in Great Chart and another in Hothfield, while the small shop in Hothfield stocks sandwiches and cold drinks.

Although this walk takes in just two ghosts, it is one of the most rewarding in the book. The route takes in a site of special interest to bird-watchers and botanists as well as offering stunning views for those more interested in scenic beauty than in details of nature. The village of Great Chart is one of the most historic in Kent, while the village churches that are included on this walk are charm itself. There is even a waterfall, albeit a manmade creation.

The Walk

1) Park in the car park that serves Hothfield Common. Travelling south along the A20, pass through Ram Lane, then bear right along the lane signposted to Hothfield. The car park is about 150 yards on the left. Leave the car park on foot and turn left along the lane.

The ghost that lurks in this gloomy, tree covered lane is that of Robert, a notorious Kent highwayman who came to a grisly end here in the early 1700s. What is now the A20 was then the Folkestone Road, and it provided rich pickings for any highwayman who fancied his chances.

The highwayman is a much celebrated figure in English folklore, and particularly in Kent where several great high roads gave such men the opportunity to practise their calling. Some highwaymen have become celebrated as friends to the poor and punishers of wealthy wrongdoers, though in reality most were simply out to steal what they could and

The tree-shaded lane where the phantom highwayman of Hothfield is seen most often.

found rich travellers more lucrative targets than poor folk. Nevertheless, the highwaymen themselves often did their best to live up to the reputation that their dishonest way of life had gained.

The earliest highwaymen, as opposed to simple highway robbers, took to the roads during the later 17th century. Typically these men were gentlemen who had lost their money and estates by supporting the doomed cause of King Charles I during the Civil Wars of the 1640s. Several such impoverished gentry earned a living in Europe as mercenaries, others took to farming or to teaching, but several became robbers. Mounted on their splendid war chargers, dressed in the finest fashions and exhibiting the courtly manners of the gentlemen they were, these early highwaymen were quickly recognised by both the public they robbed and the criminals who looked up to them as something new.

One, Captain Thomas Hind, became the subject of a hugely successful play in London in 1651 as his dishonest career reached its height. He was captured in 1652 and sent to the gallows for treason, not for robbery. Another, Captain Philip Stafford, made a point of robbing supporters of the Parliament of all they had, even their clothes, while royalists were relieved only of their ready cash. While awaiting execution in Reading Gaol in the 1660s, Stafford was visited by many of the men who had served under his command in the Civil War, and a major riot was only narrowly averted.

It was the careers of such men that Robert of Hothfield hoped to emulate. Like others who took to the road, Robert first thieved enough money to set himself up as a highwayman proper. He stole enough money to buy himself a good horse – as essential for a quick getaway as for the impression it made – and a suit of the finest clothes money could buy. Then he set off for the road to make his fortune.

Robert's peculiar talent was his charming manner and witty conversation. He would wait beside the Folkestone Road, as if pausing to eat a snack, and keep a lookout for some lone horseman who looked as if he might be worth robbing. Robert would then accost the stranger and engage him in conversation. He would warn the stranger that a highwayman was reported to be in the area and suggest they rode together as a pair of travellers would be more able to defend themselves. If the stranger agreed, Robert would ride alongside him for a while to allay any suspicions, then take advantage of a moment's inattention to whip out his weapons and force the traveller to hand over his purse and any valuables he might have.

Highwaymen rode the main roads of Kent looking for likely victims.

What made Robert Hothfield so particularly successful was that he managed to waylay several merchants and gentlemen returning from the continent with pocketfuls of cash gained from trading in Europe.

But Robert tried his trick once too often. He stopped a traveller and, as usual, suggested they ride together. What Robert did not realise was that he had robbed the same man a year or so earlier and that he had at once been

The path over Hothfield Common crosses open ground as well as passing through dense woodlands.

recognised. This time it was Robert who was taken by surprise, finding himself staring down the barrel of a pistol. The guns of the time were notoriously inaccurate and prone to misfire, so Robert decided to make a dash for it. The stranger's pistol, however, fired true and the bullet struck Robert in the back.

Robert put his spurs to his horse and rode for his home in Hothfield. He turned off the Folkestone Road and had got into this lane when death overtook him and he tumbled from his horse. His body was found later that day by a local farmer who recognised him and took his remains home to his family.

Thereafter the ghost of Robert the Highwayman was seen often trotting wearily along this lane, heading from the A20 towards Hothfield and the home he would never reach. He is dressed as one would expect in tricorn hat and embroidered coat, mounted on a fine horse. The pair plod wearily down the road, then vanish abruptly at the spot where Robert died.

In 1974, the ghost appeared in unusual form. He materialised in front of a local woman walking down this lane from her home in Tutt Hill to the shop in Hothfield. Unusually he was headless, which startled the lady considerably. Why he should have appeared in such a macabre form is unclear, he was soon back to his more usual appearance on subsequent occasions.

2) Ignore the entrance to the common opposite the southern end of the car park. Around 100 yards south of the car park, turn right through a gate to enter Hothfield Common. Walk through the woodland, then across a broad open area to meet a footpath running north-south on the edge of another patch of woodland. Turn left. This new path soon acquires a concrete surface and strikes across stagnant bogs of great botanical interest. These are the last remaining acidic bogs in Kent, the rest having long since been drained, and are now a protected nature reserve.

The bogs of Hothfield are treacherous underfoot, but are of great botanic importance.

3) Beyond the bogs, pass through a stile of the chained gate variety. At the end of the concrete path, turn left on to a path with woodland to the left and with a hedge on the right. After just 30 yards or so, turn right to cross a stile through the hedge. This stile is easy to miss as it is tucked behind a tree and masked by what appears to be a section of wire fence but is, in fact, a gate. Cross a field with a pond in it to a stile beyond. This gives access to a second field, with a stile through a hedge on the far side.

The ancient Hothfield Church stands beside the route of the walk.

4) Beyond this stile, turn sharp left to follow the edge of the field to another stile. This gives access to a wide pasture. The exit is out of sight over the crest of a hill. Walk across the field diagonally forward and right. As you crest the hill a large double gate will come into view with a small stile just to the left. Cross this stile into a lane.

5) At the lane, turn left, then right through a kissing gate to join the Greensand Way. Follow this well-signed path across open fields to another lane. Cross the lane, passing through a gate in a fine brick wall to join a surfaced path that runs to the village church of Hothfield. You can visit the church if you wish, but the Greensand Way continues across fields leaving the church on the right.

6) Continue downhill across fields, following the signs for the Greensand Way, to cross a small stream and climb uphill to emerge on to a lane at a three-way junction. Turn right, heading southwest. This quiet lane meanders southward for some distance before crossing a railway line and at once reaching a crossroads.

7) Go straight across the crossroads along a drive that leads up to Goldwell Farm. Pass through the farmyard and turn left on to the broad bridleway. This bridleway skirts the summit of Goldwell Hill, offering fine views. Follow the bridleway as it bends right and then heads for the village of Great Chart, visible in the valley ahead.

Goldwell Farm was, in the mid-15th century, the birthplace and home of James Goldwell, who became vicar of Great Chart in 1458. It was during his time as rector that much of the church was burnt down, and it remained largely in ruins for some years. In 1472 Goldwell was promoted to be Bishop of Norwich, travelling to Rome to accept the pallium of office from Pope Sixtus IV himself. Pope Sixtus was notorious for the way he promoted his nephews – the origin of the term "nepotism" – and for plundering the wealth of the papacy to benefit his own family. Sixtus happily signed an indulgence promising pardon for any sins committed during the strangely specific term of 12 years and 40 days to any who donated money to the rebuilding of the church of St Mary the Virgin at Great Chart. Armed with this indulgence, Bishop Goldwell had no trouble raising the cash to repair his old parish church.

8) The bridleway passes through the farmyard of Court Lodge, then emerges on to a lane. Turn left. The Church of St Mary the Virgin stands almost immediately on the left.

South of Hothfield, the route crosses wide open farmland.

The phantom that came to Great Chart appeared just once, but in such spectacular form that it immediately became famous and is still recognised as a remarkable apparition. On a summer's day in 1613, just as the vicar, Hadrian Savaria, began his sermon a gigantic black bull suddenly appeared in the middle of the church. The good folk of Great Chart were understandably terrified and there was a general move to get away from the snorting, stamping beast. The bull glared around with burning red eyes that seemed alive with malevolence, then it charged. Three men fell before its horns and pounding hooves before the monstrous bull hit the North Wall and exploded into a ball of hellfire which demolished part of the wall, singed the good Rev. Savaria and left behind it a curious odour.

The driveway up to Goldwell Farm, once home to a boy who became a famous cleric.

It has been suggested that the destructive bull of Great Chart was an example of the entirely natural phenomenon known today as ball lightning. This occurs usually during thundery weather when a small mass of super-charged air turns into an electric plasma, appearing as a floating globe of burning air. When the globe touches an object that connects it to earth it explodes with a vivid flash and deafening crash. Such a theory holds that the reports of the bull were mere colouring added after the event by the terrified villagers.

Such an idea might, indeed, explain the explosion, the fire and the odour. But it cannot explain the fact that in 1983 what may have been the spectral bull put in a return visit. In this case the creature was described as being a huge black dog covered with shaggy fur and with red eyes glowing with an inner fire. It was seen trotting up the lane into Great Chart from

The church tower at Great Chart, the scene of a remarkable and most unusual phantom event

the northeast, heading toward the church. The four people who saw the monstrous dog were in a car travelling in the opposite direction. The beast loomed up out of the dense mist that covered the village that evening, then trotted away, being swallowed up in the mist again.

9) Leave the churchyard and turn left along the high street of Great Chart. Just beyond a crossroads, where the road leaves the village to enter open countryside, the Greensand Way peels off along a footpath to the left. It was about here that the great black dog was seen. The well-signed path crosses open fields, then crosses the railway before dropping downhill to the Great Stour river. Ignore the path turning left, this is the Stour Valley Walk, and instead cross the stream to climb the hillside beyond towards distant woodland.

10) Continue to follow the signed route of the Greensand Way as it curves westward through woodland and across open fields. The path eventually emerges on to a narrow lane in woodland. Turn left along the narrow lane, following the lane past a small waterfall on the right.

The village sign of Great Chart dominates the High Street where a gigantic phantom hound has been seen.

11) Beyond the waterfall the lane enters Hothfield village. Bear right as you enter the village. At an off-centre crossroads, go straight on and enter woodland. If you turn left at this crossroads you will find the pub and village shop just a hundred yards on the left. Just over 300 yards along this lane is the Hothfield Common Car Park, on the right.

Walk No.10

Minster

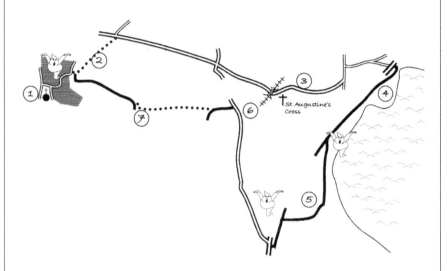

St Augustine's Cross

The gates to the ancient minster that gives this village its name.

Minster

Distance:	**8 miles**
Ghostly Rating:	* * *
Route:	**Minster - Cliffs End - Ebbsfleet - Minster**
Map:	**OS Explorer 150**
Start/Parking:	**St Mary the Virgin, Minster**
Public Transport:	**Minster has a railway station just south of the church.**
Conditions:	**Much of this walk follows the national cycle route known as the Viking Shore Route and, as a result, the paths have been upgraded to a smooth surface suitable for cycling. Elsewhere the route crosses open farmland, but nowhere is the surface difficult and there are no steep hills.**
Refreshments:	**There are two pubs in Minster which serve meals and a small shop at which soft drinks, crisps and the like may be purchased. Cliffs End has a pub on the seafront and a small shop.**

Ghosts apart, this is one of the most historic walks in the book. No less than two successful invasions of Britain came ashore at Ebbsfleet, and this walk passes by impressive monuments commemorating each of them. The ghosts are rather more enigmatic, though no less steeped in history. The walk runs along the coast for some distance, but for most of its course runs through fairly flat farmland which has been reclaimed from salt marsh over the years. The skyline to the south is dominated by the power station and wind farm of Richborough, while that to the north is filled by Kent International Airport - the former RAF Manston that saw so much action during the Battle of Britain.

The Walk

The walk begins at St Mary's Church, one of the most ancient and historic in Kent. It was founded in 670 by Ermenburga, a princess from the Kent royal family, as a nunnery of which she became the first abbess. Only a short section of wall and a doorway in the north aisle remain of this early building, but the bulk of the church is still nine centuries old and amply rewards a visit.

The foundation came at a time of upheaval in the English Church. The royal house of Kent had been the first in England to convert to Christianity some 80 years earlier, but still counted the pagan god Woden among its official ancestors and many rural communities continued with pagan practices and worship. Even among the Christians there was dispute and a heresy known as monotheism was widespread, though not common. When Archbishop Deusdedit of Canterbury died in 664 there were six years of confusion before Pope Vitalinus sent an Italian priest named Theodore to take Deusdedit's place and sort out the English church.

Theodore encouraged Ermenburga to found her nunnery at Minster. He went on to restore order to the English church by a series of compromises and agreements that were to survive until the Norman conquest.

1) Leave St Mary's Church and turn right, crossing the churchyard to emerge into the main street.

The streets of Minster are haunted by a lady dressed in grey. Unusually for a village so steeped in ecclesiastical history, this is not a nun nor any religious figure. Instead she is the ghost of a tragic lady who lived at Cleve Court, a private house in the northern part of the village. She lived during the mid-18th century and was married to the owner of Cleve Court, a most unpleasant character by all accounts.

The lady loved children, but was unable to have any of her own. Instead she lavished her affection on the children of the village, giving them little treats and always finding time to chat to them when she met them in the street. Her husband, however, grew to detest his wife's obsession and believed she was spending too much of her time and his money on the village waifs. He locked her in Cleve Court, where she soon died of a broken heart.

The kindly grey lady of Minster is seen only by children.

It is the gentle ghost of this lady who potters around the streets of Minster, though she can be seen only by children. She takes as much interest in toddlers and young children now as she did when alive, smiling gently at them and nodding happily as they play. More than one youngster has asked their parents who is the kindly lady who comes to sit and watch them at their games.

So far as is known, the Grey Lady of Minster has been seen by an adult only once: in 1949. Lady Carson, widow of Baron Edward Carson the leader of the Ulster Unionists for twenty years to 1923, came to live in Cleve Court after her husband died. Lady Carson was one day walking up the stairs of her new home when she saw coming down them a complete stranger wearing a long grey dress. The stranger quite ignored Lady Carson's demands to know who she was, but turned aside at the landing and walked into a room in the Tudor part of the building from which there was no exit. Lady Carson followed her, but the room was entirely empty. Only when she mentioned the incident to neighbours did Lady Carson learn about the phantom Grey Lady.

2) On leaving the churchyard, turn right and after 100 yards or so the Minster Abbey appears behind a pair of iron gates on your left. This entrance is not open to the public.

Continue along the lane as it turns sharp left. When the lane then bends sharp right, the entrance to the Abbey is on the left, that to the Minster Museum straight on. Where the lane turns left again a gate straight ahead gives access to a farmyard. Follow the public footpath signs across the yard to leave along a well-surfaced path. This emerges from the farm buildings to cross an open field before plunging through a hedge by way of a gate to emerge on to a lane named Grinsell Hill. Turn right. Follow this lane across a crossroads and under a railway bridge to emerge next to St Augustine's Cross

This impressive stone monument was erected here in the late 19th century to mark the spot where, according to local belief, St Augustine landed in 597 to convert the English from paganism to Christianity. The site is now some distance from the sea, but is the first spot of high land. It is possible that what now forms the flat land running to the coast was then salt marsh and that this spot is where the men sent by King Ethelbert of Kent to meet Augustine were waiting. It would certainly have

The path from Minster crosses a field and passes through a dense hedgerow.

made for a convenient location from which to keep an eye open for any ships approaching from the continent. Augustine was assured of a warm welcome for Ethelbert's queen, Bertha, was a Christian princess of the Franks who had persuaded her husband to welcome the Christian missionaries and allow them to preach the gospel. Augustine went on to be appointed the first Archbishop of Canterbury in 601 and before his death in 604 had set in motion the conversion of the southern English.

3) Continue along the lane, past the cross, to reach the little village of Cliffs End. The lane bends left, passing a post office and shop, then bends right. Soon after this take the right hand fork in the road to reach the A256 with the sea beyond. Cross the A256 and a small stretch of grass to turn right along a well-surfaced cycleway and footpath. A short distance along the path a large wooden ship is visible, raised permanently on concrete blocks.

This is the Hugin Ship, built in Denmark and rowed over the North Sea in 1949 to celebrate the 1,500th anniversary of an event that changed the history of Britain and of Europe – and has left its ghostly mark on this area. The year 449 was the date cited in the earliest

St Augustine's Cross marks the traditional spot where the Italian monk waded ashore to begin his task of converting the pagan English to Christianity.

St Augustine baptises King Ethelbert of Kent as a Christian. This was to be the highlight of Augustine's achievements.

histories for the coming of the English to Britain. They came at first as mercenaries hired by the Romano-British, but later rebelled and stayed as invaders. It has since become clear that Germanic mercenaries had been living in Britain for some generations before 449 and it is now thought that the date refers to the arrival of the brothers Hengist and Horsa, who would later lead the English rebellion.

The Hugin Ship is based largely on that of the Vikings, with its round rowlocks, high dragon-shaped figurehead and great length. Archaeology has since revealed that the English ships were rather shorter, had simple prong rowlocks and lacked a figurehead. Nevertheless, it is an impressive monument to an event of enormous historic importance. If the ghosts are to believed, however, it is not quite in the right place. As we shall see.

4) From the ship continue along the path until a pub is visible on the right. This is the spot where the old gibbet once stood.

The gibbet stood between the road and the sea, where it would be visible to travellers by land and on ship. It is thought to have stood here for generations until it was taken down in the late 18th century. It is not known how many men ended their lives swinging from the rope on this windblown spot, but it must have been several dozen over the years. After being cut down the bodies that were not claimed by relatives for a decent burial were simply tossed into a shallow grave beside the road, as were suicides forbidden burial in consecrated ground.

No doubt it is one of these unhappy folk, whose mortal remains lie just below the surface, who is causing the supernatural trouble. The most noticeable manifestation is a glowing figure that stands beside the road late at night. It is rarely seen before midnight, and just as rarely before dawn. The small hours seem the spectre's favourite time to go out haunting.

Less obviously supernatural, though

The Hugin Ship commemorates the landing of the first English settlers to arrive on these shores, near Ebbsfleet.

The bleak stretch of coast where the gibbet once stood and where ghostly events still take place.

perhaps more dangerous, is the accident record on this short stretch of road. Anywhere else and it may have gone unremarked, but combined with the glowing entity by the old gibbet site it becomes quite unnerving. The road here is quite straight and there are no difficult junctions or turnings. And yet an unusually large number of minor accidents and crashes take place here. The drivers do not report any particular reason - there is no sudden ghostly apparition to make them lose control of their vehicles. There are just a lot of accidents.

5) Continue along the path to a car park. In the car park, bear left off the surfaced track to join a footpath along the coast that leaves the car park beside a large wooden litter bin. Follow this path around the coast, then as it bends to the right inland along the edge of extensive stretches of salt marsh. These mark the mouth of the River Stour, visible as a thin silver streak amid the marshes in sunny weather. In August and September this stretch of path is lined by brambles bearing large, juicy

The modern signpost that has taken the place of the old gibbet.

blackberries. When the path meets a broad gravel track at a T-junction, turn left. Follow this track until it emerges on to the A256. Cross the A256 and go straight ahead along Ebbsfleet Lane.

The ghosts that haunt these fields are reported in recent years to be vague and insubstantial, but they were not always so. Today these spectres are grey misty shapes that glide over the grass, slip behind bushes, come together and dissipate in total silence. Older accounts going back many years state that this is the site of hauntings by a group of big,

muscular men armed with spears and carrying round shields. It has been surmised that these are the phantoms of Hengist, Horsa and their English warriors wading ashore in Britain for the first time. It may be so, for Ebbsfleet is the traditional site of their landing. If this be the case, and both history and ghosts indicate it is, then the impressive ship at Cliffs End is in the wrong place.

The coast path that skirts the salt flats of Ebbsfleet.

Perhaps the ghosts know best, but their wispy nature makes it unlikely that they will tell.

6) Continue along Ebbsfleet Lane until it reaches a level crossing. Turn left just before the railway on to a farm track which heads almost exactly due west. After about 200 yards the track divides in two, each branch going through a gate. Take the right hand gate, and follow the edge of the field as the track rapidly dwindles into a footpath.

7) When the path meets a surfaced farm track, turn right to cross a level crossing. Follow the track as it strikes leftward up a gentle slope to the now visible spire of Minster Church. As the track approaches a cottage and the farmyard, it turns sharp right. Go straight on through a line of bollards and between some houses to emerge back into the main street of Minster. The Abbey is on your right and the church straight ahead of you.

The dense brambles of Ebbsfleet are heavy with berries in the late summer months.

The field at Ebbsfleet where shadowy figures may recreate an historic landing.

Where the pathway divides beside the railway north of Ebbsfleet, the walker needs to bear right.

Walk No.11

Saltwood

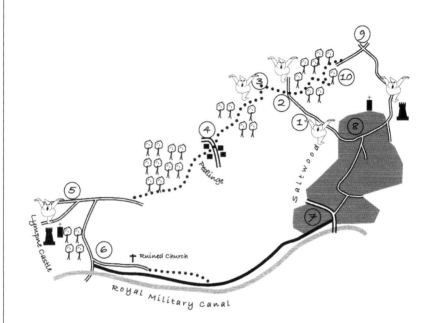

The village sign of Saltwood celebrates its castle and its forests.

Saltwood

Distance:	8 miles
Ghostly Rating:	* * * * * *
Route:	Saltwood - Lympne - West Hythe - Saltwood
Map:	OS Explorer 138
Start/Parking:	Brockhill Country Park car park, Saltwood
Public Transport:	The walk starts at the car park, located just 300 yards south of Sandling Railway Station.
Conditions:	A walk that involves sweeping sea views, open countryside and dense forests. There are several steep hills and in places the path is rather rough and the surface broken, but otherwise the going is good and firm.
Refreshments:	The walk passes two pubs in Saltwood, and another pub is just a few yards off the route in Lympne.

This is one of the most energetic walks in this book, involving steep climbs up and down the slopes of the South Downs. The effort is rewarded by sweeping views across the Downs and out over the Straits of Dover. The supernatural is never far away from the walker on this route, with the atmospheric ruins and remains of the past providing a suitable backdrop to the unusual tales of ghosts and phantoms.

The Walk

1) Park in the Brockhill Country Park car park just south of Sandling railway station on the lane that runs from Saltwood to Sandling. Brockhill is signposted from the A20 and the A261. Leave the car park to find yourself on the Sandling Road. Look to your right.

This stretch of road is the haunt of two ghosts - or possibly just the one. The first is by far the more gentle of the two. This is of an elderly lady dressed in a sensible tweed suit who

The terrifying apparition that appeared in this field caused four teenagers to take to their heels.

The footbridge over the Slay Brook stream where a misty phantom has been seen.

is out walking her little dog. Those who have seen this particular phantom report that she is at once both quite ordinary and yet noticeably odd. She appears quite solid and real in all respects, not semi-transparent nor floating above the pavement, and yet she attracts attention by some indefinable strangeness.

This is not at all unusual for a ghost. Despite what fiction writers or film makers might have us believe, ghosts are more often solid than not. Some people do, indeed, mistake them for real people until they vanish or otherwise behave oddly. And yet there is always something strange about them. Perhaps the shadows are not quite right. Or they are in bright sunshine, when it is in reality a cloudy day. Whatever it is, there is something odd about this quiet lady and her dog that attracts attention as she wanders down the lane and into Brockhill Country Park.

The second phantom is altogether more dramatic and alarming. This is the ghost of a woman who steps off the pavement straight into the path of oncoming vehicles. More than one driver has slammed on their brakes or swerved to one side, desperate to avoid a collision with the mysterious figure. Descriptions of this phantom are vague. She is seen for only a second or two and the drivers are understandably more concerned with avoiding a crash than noticing what the person looks like.

There are some who think the two phantoms might be one and the same. Perhaps the old lady in tweeds crosses the road, and causes alarm and shock as she does so. It is, after all, more likely that the same ghost is responsible than that there are two different ghosts on the same stretch of road.

The clear signage around Saltwood make the route easy to follow.

2) Walk northwest along Sandling Road towards Sandling. After a hundred yards or so the road bends to the right while a kissing gate on the left gives access to a path, signposted as the Saxon Shore Way. Continue forwards about 25 yards on the lane until an open field sloping upwards is seen on your left.

This was the scene of a most peculiar event on 16 November 1963. Four teenagers were walking from Saltwood to the railway station at Sandling along this road just as the early autumnal dusk was closing in. The four consisted of two boys from the village who were walking their girlfriends to the station as the first leg of their journey home.

As the youngsters came around this corner one of the boys happened to glance across the field. He saw a bright light moving among the trees and pointed it out to his friends. The object seemed to hover about, then faded from view. A few seconds later a figure came shambling out of the wood and started across the field towards them. It fell down, picked itself up and kept on coming. The teenagers were alarmed to see that it seemed to be entirely black and to have a pair of wings instead of arms. Even worse, they could see no head. Without waiting to discover what this thing was, they fled.

One of the boys, named John, later told a reporter from the local press. "There was a silhouette which fell down heavily. Then got up. It was very black and about the size of a man, but it had no head. It appeared to have wings on either side of the body – like a bat. It came towards us, stumbling as it came. We did not wait to find out what it was, but ran."

The story was a bit of a wonder for a while, but then interest faded. But three years later a very similar figure was seen several times in the USA. The newspapers there dubbed the apparition "The Mothman" and linked

The finely carved top of the Shepway Cross marks the way outside Lympne.

it to UFOs and flying saucers. For a while this stretch of road outside Saltwood became a focus for those interested in UFOs, but when nothing much happened interest again faded.

Although not directly on this walk, another stretch of this same road is haunted by a rather more conventional phantom. The road about a mile to the west, near Sandling Station, is

Lympne Castle plays host to some ancient ghosts, but is not always open to the public.

the haunt of a man carrying a lantern. Sometimes only the light of the lantern is seen bobbing about beside the road, but more often the man himself appears. He is thick set, wearing the clothes of a labourer from a century or so ago. He seems to be scanning the road towards Saltwood as if awaiting somebody.

3) Return to the kissing gate and follow the path along the side of an open field and into some woodland. The well-signed path goes downhill, turns sharp left and then takes a short detour to avoid a large, fallen tree. Just beyond this tree is a stout wooden bridge with a metal handrail that crosses a small stream. This is the ominously-named Slay Brook Stream that runs south to enter the sea near Hythe.

The stream took its name from a particularly unpleasant little battle that took place here almost two thousand years ago. After the Roman invasion of Britain it was some time before the locals settled down to life under their new masters. The Romans brought not just villas and piped hot water with them, they also brought new taxes, new laws and new duties, not all of which were terribly welcome among the native Cantiaci tribe of Kent. For some years there was resistance and trouble among the tribesmen as they tried to avoid paying taxes and preferred their own laws to those of Rome.

Eventually the Roman authorities decided that an example was to be made of the next village to cause trouble, and that village happened to be a settlement on the banks of this Slay Brook stream. Perhaps they refused to pay their taxes, or roughed up a Roman official. Whatever their crime, their punishment was severe. A Roman cohort came down from the fortress city of Canterbury and slaughtered the entire village of Britons. Men, women, children and elderly were all put to the sword in a dreadful orgy of bloodshed.

It is perhaps no wonder that the centurion who led the attack returns to the banks of this little stream. Is he consumed with guilt, or has he come to gloat? Nobody is quite certain. He appears most often on chill mornings as the mist rises from the stream. A tendril of vapour will swirl and solidify to form the figure of this ancient soldier, then it disperses and is gone.

4) From the bridge, follow the path past another fallen tree and uphill to leave the woodland. Cross open fields to a cluster of buildings that make up the hamlet of Pedlinge. Cross the A261 here, turning left, then right to enter what appears to be a drive leading to a farm, with a pond on the left. The path exits this drive on the right, striking across an open field to a distant stile.

5) Follow the signposted path across the fields until it emerges, by way of a rickety stile, on to the lane the links Saltwood to Lympne. Turn right along this lane, passing the impressive Shepway Cross on the left. Turn left down the narrow lane signposted to Lympne Castle. If you fancy a break here, continue straight on to find a pub, before returning to pick up the walk. At the end of this lane is found the castle and parish church.

The people of this corner of Kent seem to have been a robust lot when it came to resisting invaders. If the ghost of the Slay Brook stream harks back to the Roman invasion, one of those at Lympne has its origins during the Norman conquest of 1066.

The ghosts, there are six of them in total, are seen in and near the West Tower of the castle. These men were priests in Kent in that fateful year of 1066 and they were married. This was quite in order in England at the time, but was severely frowned upon by the Pope. England, however, did not care much. Although part of the universal Christian Church administered by the Pope from Rome, the English had for centuries had some indiosyncratic customs that dated back to the time when the older Celtic Church, that had survived the pagan invasions, was merged with that of Rome.

Pope Alexander II in Rome did not much appreciate the English Church having its own ways. Even less did he like the fact that the English did not send as much silver and gold to Rome as he thought they should. So when King Edward of England died without a son and heir, the Pope was delighted. He promised to give papal blessing to one of the claimants to the throne on condition that the English Church be made firmly subject to Rome. That candidate was William, Duke of Normandy, and he duly went on to conquer England.

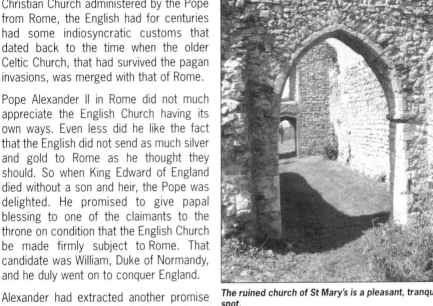

The ruined church of St Mary's is a pleasant, tranquil spot.

Alexander had extracted another promise from William. This was that Alexander's old schoolmaster, Lanfranc of Bec, should be appointed Archbishop of Canterbury. Partly this was to repay his old teacher, but mainly to ensure that the English Church did as it was told. When he arrived, Lanfranc was appalled to find that six of the priests in Canterbury were married. He at once arrested the hapless men and had them thrown into prison inside the newly completed Norman fortress of Lympne Castle. A few weeks later the six priests were dead. Lanfranc uttered some pious statements about their sins finding them out, but others were convinced the men had been murdered to encourage other English priests to follow the instructions from Rome.

The unfortunate priests were given a decent burial in Lympne churchyard, but their spirits could not rest. They were soon seen lurking mournfully around the stone walls that had held them prisoner, and they are seen there still.

The second ghost of Lympne is never seen. He marches across the courtyard of Lympne Castle, stomps up the steps to the top of the tower, but never comes down. For some reason the sounds he makes are said to be the footsteps of a Roman centurion who fell to his death from the tower. This is most unlikely. The tower in question was built in the 1340s and, although there was a Roman fortress at Lympne, it stood 300 yards away from the medieval castle. Whoever's ghost makes the spectral footfalls is, in reality, unknown.

Lympne Castle is now a conference centre that also plays host to weddings and other celebrations. It is open to the public when not hired for a private event.

The Royal Military Canal was built during the Napoleonic Wars, but was to have been used again in 1940 if the Germans had invaded Britain.

6) Return to the Shepway Cross. Turn right down the lane that slopes steeply towards the distant sea. At the foot of this hill, turn left before the pub to reach the ruined church of St Mary's. No ghost is attached to the romantic ruin, but it is a most atmospheric place. Return to the road, turn left past the pub and almost at once left again to join the Royal Military Canal Path, just before the bridge.

This Royal Military Canal is one of the more spectacular reminders of the dark days in the early 19th century when Britain expected invasion from the France of the Emperor Napoleon. It was designed to serve two purposes. Primarily the canal served as a route for transporting goods and people. The more usual coastal route had been made dangerous by fast-sailing French ships which would sweep down, capture or sink British coastal vessels and then race back to France before the Royal Navy could intervene. The canal allowed barges to carry such goods and people in total safety.

Its secondary purpose was to act as an obstacle to an invading army. As soon as the French landed, the bridges over the canal were to be blown up or torched. It was hoped the disruption this would cause to transport would hinder the French supply lines and slow down their advancing army. Over a century later, a very similar plan was drawn up once again. If Hitler's Germans had invaded in 1940 they would have found the bridges over the Royal Military Canal destroyed and so their transport system would have been in difficulties.

The ghostly knights who ride out from Saltwood Castle are dressed in the armour of the later 12th century.

7) As the Royal Military Canal Path enters the village of Saltwood, it emerges next to the A261. Turn left and, when the A261 turns sharp left, go straight on into Barrack Hill. Follow this road steeply uphill, turning left into Bartholomew Lane and following this road until it emerges on to the small village green, flanked by a welcoming pair of pubs.

8) Cross the small green, and turn right along Grange Road. At the end of this road, bear left into the narrower lane. Almost immediately on your right is the entrance to Saltwood Castle.

Just a hundred years after the events that led to the hauntings at Lympne, relations between the King of England and the Pope had collapsed - which led to a new haunting in Saltwood. The Church had used the privileges and powers granted by William I to build up its wealth and independence from the state. King Henry II believed things had gone too far and that his kingdom was being stripped of cash for the benefit of the Church. His quarrels with Thomas Becket, Archbishop of Canterbury, grew worse and more violent as the years passed and each new crisis added to the distrust between the two.

As so often in long-running disputes of principle, the final crisis came over a minor incident. A servant of King Henry, Robert de Broc, was caught hunting in a wood that belonged to the Church. Thomas Becket preached a sermon in Canterbury Cathedral in which he condemned thieves and excommunicated de Broc. Henry was in France when he

The lane that runs north from Saltwood is so quiet that grass grows along the centre of the roadway.

heard the news. He lost his temper in dramatic fashion. He raged and swore, then turned on his knights and shouted "What sluggards and knaves have I fed in my house that they are faithless to their lord. Will nobody rid me of this turbulent priest?"

Four of the knights – William de Tracy, Hugh de Moreville, Reginald FitzUrse and Richard the Breton – took the words seriously and set off for England. They made straight for Saltwood Castle, then owned by de Broc's brother Reginald. There the four knights plotted their next move. Thomas was in Canterbury dealing with the administration of church lands. The four men decided to arrive shortly after dinner so as to catch Thomas in his business chambers.

In mid-morning on 29 December the four knights donned their armour, picked up their swords – FitzUrse chose a battleaxe – and mounted their horses. They trotted out of the gateway, into what is now Grange Road and turned right up the hill towards Canterbury.

Despite their plans, when the knights caught up with him Thomas was inside the holy cathedral. After vainly trying to first persuade, then drag the archbishop off holy ground, the knights attacked. William de Tracy struck first, but it was Richard the Breton who dealt the fatal blow.

The murder sent shock waves throughout Christendom, and has left its spectral mark in several places in Kent. Canterbury Cathedral is haunted by Thomas Becket himself, while the little church at Kemsing is visited by the penitent ghost of one of the murderers who stopped here after the crime in remorse at his acts. At Saltwood, the hauntings take two forms. For many years there was an oak table in the castle around which, it was said, the knights had plotted the crime. It was marked by a strange blood stain that could not be removed by even the most diligent scrubbing. And on 29th December each year the stain grew wet with blood.

The road outside the castle gates is likewise best visited on the anniversary of the murder. Around 11am, the sound of pounding horses' hooves may be heard coming out of the castle gates and heading up the hill. The ghosts are never seen, but there can be no doubt that these are the phantoms of the murderers off to do their grisly business. Saltwood Castle is a private home and is not open to the public.

9) Continue up the steep hill to reach a crossroads. Turn left down the poorly made up lane that leads downhill towards a fruit farm. After 300 yards the lane divides into three, bear right. Follow this path through woodlands.

10) Just after the path passes a steep slope dropping away on the left, it is crossed by a path at an old stile, now disused as the fence it once crossed has been removed. Turn sharp right, passing to the right of the stile. Follow this path downhill, turning left when it reaches the edge of the woodland. Follow the edge of the woodland, bearing left to pick up the path when it appears to peter out at one point. The path continues downhill across open land, then plunges again into dense woodland before crossing a small stream and abruptly emerging on to the Sandling Road. Turn left to return to the car park.

The path back to the car park cross open glades amid the dense forest.

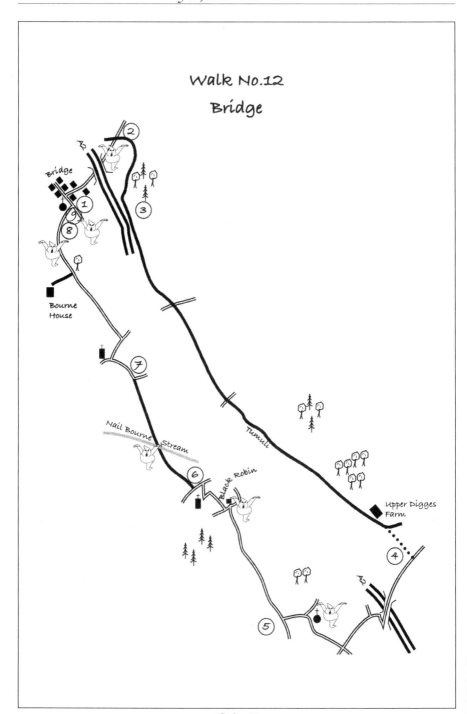

Walk No.12

Bridge

Bridge

Distance:	9 miles
Ghostly Rating:	* * * * * *
Route:	Bridge - Patrixbourne - Barham - Kingston - Bishopsbourne - Bridge
Map:	OS Explorer 150 and 138
Start/Parking:	Bridge
Conditions:	Most of this walk follows the well signposted North Downs Way and the Elham Valley Way, both of which are well maintained paths, but can be muddy in places.
Refreshments:	There are several pubs along the route that offer tempting menus, and a shop in Bridge sells soft drinks and snacks.

This walk begins with a stiff climb up on to the windswept heights of the Barham Downs, but once there the going is fairly even with fine views across the valley of the Nail Bourne stream that flows northward to Canterbury. A second steep slope leads down into the valley, after which the walk runs along level ground in the valley which is undemanding, but can be muddy in places.

The Walk

1) From Bridge high street, take the lane that heads northeast just north of the bridge over the Nail Bourne stream, signposted to "Patrixbourne". Follow the lane as it passes under the modern A2 dual carriageway.

This road is haunted by possibly the most famous ghost in Kent, though there are few who realise it appears as a phantom. Indeed, some do not believe that the thing ever existed at all. The car Chitty Chitty Bang Bang has featured in books, stage plays and a film. Although the magical flying abilities of the car are pure fiction, the car itself was real enough and dominated the world of motor racing in the early 1920s.

The lanes east of Bridge are haunted by a famous phantom car.

The car was the invention of a flamboyant Hungarian, Count Louis Zobrowski, who made his home in Patrixbourne after the collapse of the Austro-Hungarian Empire in the wake of the First World War. The Count had always been interested in the exciting new sport of motor racing and was determined to create an unbeatable racing car. He therefore brought to this little English village a selection of car chassis, engines and a talented team of mechanics.

In 1920 Zobrowksi startled his neighbours by taking to the road in a Mercedes chassis to which he had attached a 23 litre Zeppelin engine, two seats and minimal coachwork of timber and hand-beaten metal sheeting. The astonishingly powerful car was amazingly fast, though it had trouble on corners, and was dubbed Chitty Chitty Bang Bang by its proud creator.

In its very first race the car became the first to average 100mph in a contest. And in its second race astounded onlookers by topping 120mph. Zobrowski was delighted. He dressed his mechanics in identical uniforms, something then unheard of, and adopted a fanciful version of traditional Hungarian folk costume for his own public appearances. The car, he liked to boast, went so fast it seemed to fly.

For two years Zobrowski and Chitty Chitty Bang Bang reigned supreme, but then other drivers and mechanics began to catch up. The Count retired his great car from racing and brought it back to Patrixbourne where he used it to take visitors on exhilarating drives around the countryside. He particularly liked to race down this long, straight lane to show off the car's extraordinary turn of speed.

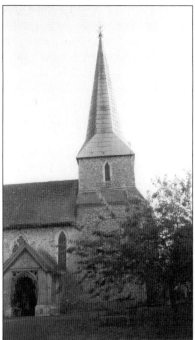

In 1924 the Count agreed to drive a car belonging to the Mercedes team in a race at Monza, in Italy. The car crashed and the Count was killed. His family sold off his remaining cars, or broke them up for scrap. The great Chitty Chitty Bang Bang being one of those dismantled. But just a few weeks later the Count and his famous car were seen again, racing down this stretch of road at incredible speed. He is still seen, from time to time, belting along with scarf streaming out behind him. Perhaps it was here that he was happiest, racing his great car around the lovely lanes of Kent.

2) Continue along the lane until a stile on the right gives access to an open field. The path forms part of the North Downs Way, and is signposted as such. Follow the direction of the signpost steeply uphill toward a wood. The path then turns right to run along the face of the wood. At the far end of the wood, the path turns sharp left to run along the top of the cutting in which runs the modern A2.

The little church at Barham is frequented by a tranquil, unassuming ghost.

3) The path follows the side of the A2 for a short

distance, then strikes off left across open fields, over a country lane and past an orchard towards a radio mast beside a second lane. Cross this lane, still following the well signposted North Downs Way. A short distance past the radio mast a cluster of prehistoric burial mounds is visible on the right.

This stretch of high, open ground where the burial mounds are situated is called the Barham Downs. Located between Canterbury and Dover, and offering plenty of space close to water and fodder, the downs have long attracted armies. The Romans camped here on their way inland to conquer Britain, and William the Conqueror rested his army here after the Battle of Hastings in 1066. Roundheads and Cavaliers both camped here during the Civil War of the 1640s, and the Grand Old Duke of York of nursery rhyme fame stopped here before his ill-fated invasion of France in the 1790s.

Few ghosts are commemorated in such solid form as is the ghost of the Black Robin pub.

Of all the visitors however, only one man has listened to the local legends about the burial mounds and taken them seriously. That man was King Henry VIII. As soon as he heard local peasants talking about a life-sized statue made of solid gold that is supposedly buried here, the king ordered the mounds to be excavated. His engineers went to work and in the very first mound opened discovered the skeleton of some long-dead warrior dressed in armour decorated with gold leaf. Assuming the locals had been talking about this burial, Henry called off his diggers and marched on to Dover on his way to meet the King of France.

4) Continue along the North Downs Way past the burial mounds to Upper Digges Farm. Beyond the farm buildings the North Downs Way veers to the left. Continue straight on along a footpath that crosses an open field to reach a lane beside a small wood. Turn right along this lane to cross the busy A2 dual carriageway by means of a bridge. Continue along the lane to a crossroads, turning right to enter the village of Barham. The church of St John the Baptist stands on the right, just as you enter the village.

The ghost that lurks in the churchyard is a quiet soul. She is dressed in the fashions of the early 19th century and potters around the churchyard as if out for a gentle stroll. Nobody knows who this ghost might be, but she appears to be aged around 30 or so and some report she carries a small posy of flowers. Perhaps she is carrying it to place on the grave of some beloved, or on her own.

5) Past the church, follow the lane as it bends left down the hill through Barham village. The lane reaches a crossroads beside a pub. Turn right. This lane runs northward with broad grass verges to a T-junction. In front of you is the Black Robin pub.

The pub is named after Black Robin himself, a colourful highwayman who enjoyed great

The haunted bar at the Black Robin has played host to some impressive ghostly carousing and merrymaking.

success around here in the 1750s. He robbed travellers on the Dover Road, now the A2, and for some years seemed to lead a charmed life. The secret of his success was his patriotism. Black Robin held up only foreigners, preferring not to rob Englishmen and never on any account taking a penny from a native of Kent. As a result, the locals had no real incentive to inform the authorities that Black Robin spent much of his time in this inn, where he was courting the landlord's daughter.

But it could not last forever. Finally, Black Robin was caught, hauled away in chains and hanged for his crimes. When the landlord's daughter heard of his capture, she locked herself in the cellar of the inn, weeping inconsolably for days on end. She died of a broken heart soon afterward.

But that was not the last that the inn had heard of Black Robin, nor of the landlord's daughter. Before long the distinctive sounds of Black Robin's horse trotting into the courtyard began to be heard late at night, and then Black Robin himself would stride into the inn before vanishing into thin air. And sometimes the faint sounds of the girl weeping would echo up the cellar steps.

Both phantoms continue to visit

The Black Robin pub is a welcoming stop, but it was tragedy that led to the hauntings of this jovial place.

the Black Robin to this day. Black Robin most recently appeared in 2003, when he rode into the courtyard, but vanished before entering the pub. As if to make up for the phantom's oversight, the landlady has acquired a tailor's dummy and dressed it in the distinctive clothes of Black Robin. The figure now stands by the bar, greeting visitors to his favourite haunt.

6) At the T-junction turn left, then immediately right to enter the village of Kingston. This lane twists left then right past the church before reaching a T-junction. Turn left. After 50 yards, take a bridlepath on the right between two houses that is signposted as being the

The coming of Christianity to the valley of the Nail Bourne stream led to a conflict with the old gods which has left its spectral mark in the Kent countryside.

Elham Valley Way. This well-marked route crosses one field, enters another and then crosses the Nail Bourne stream by way of a footbridge.

This stream is deceptive. For most of the time it is a quiet little affair babbling gently between its banks as it runs downhill to join the Little Stour, and then the Great Stour some miles east of Canterbury. But on rare occasions it becomes a boiling torrent in flood as heavy rains pound the downs, throwing vast quantities of water into the Nail Bourne.

Legend has it that the stream floods once every seven years as a result of supernatural activity. In the summer of 597, just after he had arrived in Kent to convert the pagan English, St Augustine came to this valley to preach the Gospel of Christ. The local pagans listened politely to the stranger. When he had finished they asked if his new God could do something useful, like provide some water to halt the drought that was threatening their crops. St Augustine duly knelt in prayer. When he stood up the prints left by his knees filled with water, that rapidly overflowed, tumbling into the dry bed of the Nail Bourne to fill the stream with precious water. The locals flocked around the saint in gratitude and turned to Christianity.

The coming of Christianity to the valley of the Nail Bourne stream led to a conflict with the old gods which has left its spectral mark in the Kent countryside.

The old pagan gods were, as might be guessed, displeased. As soon as St Augustine had returned to Canterbury, they came racing down the valley in anger and fury. A great wind tore up trees and flattened houses. Then the rains came, heavier than any mortal had ever seen. Within minutes a flash flood was pouring down the valley. If the old gods thought they would win back their worshippers, they were mistaken. Augustine returned in a great hurry and threw himself down in prayer to God. It was a titanic struggle, but eventually St Augustine overcame the pagan gods and their fury. But he could not defeat them entirely. Once every seven years the old gods break free, bringing floods and turmoil to the valley of the Nail Bourne.

The old gods last wrought their anger in the autumn of 2002. They are due to return, therefore, in 2009.

7) Beyond the footbridge, the route runs along the left edge of a field before joining a track that runs beside the stream and into the little village of Bishopsbourne. As the track enters the village it joins a lane that comes in from the right. Go straight ahead through the village and past the pub. Just before the church, turn sharp right and then left into Bourne Park Road. About half a mile along this lane the entrance to Bourne House is on the left.

This historic house is now the Bridge Country Club, but its ghost dates back to the days when it was a private house. A serving girl here in the 1780s had the misfortune to be seduced by the master of the house, whose passion turned to coldness when the girl became pregnant. The baby was born, but died shortly afterward. It was the gossip in the villages nearby that the master of the house had smothered the inconvenient infant. Be that as it may, he certainly refused to pay for a decent funeral.

The poor mother had to carry her dead child in a linen basket from the grand house along this lane to the church in Bridge to be placed in a pauper's grave. The girl then left Bridge, never to return. It was presumed she had gone to stay with relatives far enough away that the scandal would not follow her. It is to be hoped that she was happy.

And yet, some years later, the girl returned in ghostly form to retrace that sad journey from Bourne House to Bridge Church. The phantom cradled gently in her arms a linen basket, covered by a simple white cloth. She is seen most often as dusk draws in, drifting slowly along, her precious load in her arms and her head bowed in sorrow.

8) Continue along Bourne Park Road as it bends gently to the right. At a T-junction look up the hill to your right.

You are looking at the old A2, now downgraded, as the modern dual carriageway bypasses the village. Before it was the A2 it was the Dover Road, and before that it was the main Roman highway from Dubris (Dover) to Durovernum Cantiaci (Canterbury). And before that it was a Celtic track. Down this road sometimes hurtles a Celtic war chariot, the ponies racing at full gallop as they are urged on by the driver and the warrior standing behind resplendent in war paint and brightly coloured clothes. This startling apparition is seen rarely, and then only for a few seconds, but clearly enough for more than one witness to give a detailed description.

Clearly the Celtic warrior is in a great rush to get somewhere, perhaps to a battle. But who he is and whether he rides so furiously to take part in a tribal conflict or to oppose the might of Rome, we do not know.

9) Turn left at the T-junction to return back to the village of Bridge.

Walk No.13
Chilham

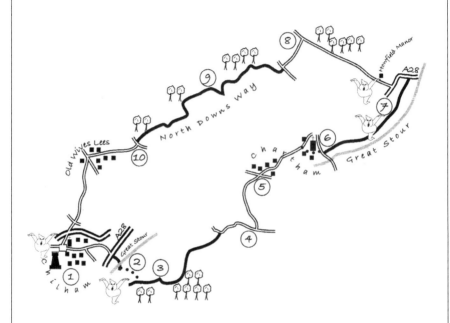

The main square at Chilham is surrounded by ancient houses – and by ghosts.

Chilham

Distance:	10 miles
Ghostly Rating:	* * * * * *
Route:	Chilham - Chartham - Horton - Chartham Hatch - Old Wives Lees - Chilham
Map:	OS Explorer 149 & 150
Start/Parking:	Chilham
Public Transport:	The walk starts in the village square of Chilham. Chilham Railway Station is outside the village to the east. Leave the station, turn left along the main road to pick up the walk at Point 2.
Conditions:	This walk clambers up and down steep hills, traverses narrow woodland paths and, in places, can be muddy in wet weather. Other sections are along country lanes that offer easy going.
Refreshments:	The walk passes two pubs in Chilham, one in Chartham and a fourth in Chartham Hatch, all of which serve meals. There is a shop in Chilham and another in Chartham that offer soft drinks and light snacks.

This is a long and, at times, fairly strenuous walk. In most places, however, the surface is good and the hills reward the walker with some impressive views across the Stour Valley and over the Kentish hills. It is one of the more scenically rewarding as well as strenuous paths in this book. The ghosts to be encountered are an active lot which remain able to startle even those who know that they exist.

The Walk

The walk starts in the main square which stands at the heart of the hilltop village of Chilham. This square is the location of three staples of the English countryside: Church, castle and pub. Two of the three are haunted.

The castle is a private home which is open to the public infrequently, though it does play host to corporate dinners and other events and the gardens are open on several weekends in the summer. The ghosts here can be very active, but are not especially frightening. That seen most often is the ghost of a young woman dressed in medieval clothes who walks

The church at Chilham, it is a phantom former vicar who is the most active ghost in the village.

around the grounds and in the Norman keep, all that remains of the medieval castle. This young lady is so realistic that many visitors to the grounds mistake her for a member of staff in period costume, and complain that she does not respond to their questions.

The second haunting occurs in and around the ladies toilet inserted into one room of the magnificent mansion built by Inigo Jones in 1616. Ladies attending corporate events or weddings have reported hearing sounds, much like that of heavy furniture being dragged around or toppling over with a heavy crash coming from the room above the toilet, even when the chamber in question is totally empty.

Across the village square from the castle is the White Horse pub. Back in the 17th century this building was the vicarage for the adjacent church, and so was home to the fiery preacher Sampson Horne. This Horne was an outspoken puritan who despised the fripperies and ceremonies favoured by King Charles I. He was an enthusiastic supporter of the austere Christianity favoured during the rule of Oliver Cromwell which followed the execution of Charles I and the Civil Wars of the 1640s.

But in 1660 the times changed and young King Charles II came to the throne. He brought with him a more relaxed and tolerant form of Christianity that met with the ire of strict puritans, such as the Rev Horne of Chilham. Horne, however, went further than most in his complaints. He condemned the new king and his ministers as ungodly and predicted God's anger would rain down upon them.

His words could have been taken as inciting rebellion, civil war or regicide, so the Archbishop of Canterbury quickly removed Horne from the post of vicar of Chilham. But Horne had money in his own right and refused to leave his home. He remained in Chilham until his death in 1677, when he was buried in the churchyard. It was not long before his ghost returned to his old home, now the White Horse.

The ghost of the elderly man in plain black clothes is seen most often near the inglenook fireplace at the rear of the ground floor. He does not bother anyone, and seems strangely content that his old home is now an inn.

1) Leave the square by the south-east corner, having turned left on leaving the White Horse pub. Follow this lane downhill past the older houses of the village. Near the bottom of the hill, the Woolpack Inn is on your right.

The owners of this welcoming pub are fully conversant with the mysteries of the internet and advertise their hostelry on a number of websites. It is, they proudly announce, "one of the cosiest inns in Kent, if not in England, with a well-kept cellar",

The rear bar at the White Horse Inn, where the ghost is seen most often.

complete with four-poster beds and traditional decor in their upstairs rooms. The ghost here is of a mysterious grey lady. Nobody seems very clear who she may be, but she is described as being "a resident but friendly ghost" by the manager.

2) Continue along the lane, ignoring turnings to the right, until the lane almost reaches the busy A252. The lane then bends right past some houses to emerge on to the equally busy A28 opposite a car repair garage. Cross the A28 with care and walk up the driveway to the left of the garage. This goes across the railway at a level crossing, then over the Great Stour by way of two bridges. After the second bridge the drive ends abruptly at a private house. Turn left along the river bank to follow a narrow path into a patch of woodland. In the woodland you will meet a broader track crossing the path at right angles. Turn right up this track to enter an open field. The long barrow is just on the right, hidden in a patch of scrub and trees.

This ancient burial mound was constructed over 4,000 years ago when Stone age farmers lived here, growing their crops on the thin, easily worked soils of the Kent chalklands. It has long been held to be a haunt of the little people, and best avoided. These are no happy-go-lucky fairies with gossamer dresses and caps made from bluebells, such as may be found in modern children's books. These are the old fairies of England, powerful and half-magical folk who have ways of their own. It is best not to annoy the little people by intruding too obviously on to their ground. Perhaps, after all, the barrow is best avoided.

The peasants of Chilham set off for London to join the great Peasants' Revolt of 1381.

3) Return to the junction and turn right, continuing along the original path. This soon emerges from the woodland on to a broad, open field. Turn left, skirting the edge of the field. When the edge of the field

The Woolpack lies just outside Chilham, but has not escaped the village's ghostly atmosphere.

suddenly turns left, continue straight on along what was clearly a hedgerow until it was grubbed out. The path appears to vanish as it approaches a patch of woodland, but continue straight on and an opening in the apparently solid wall of green will become clear. Pass through this opening and you will find yourself on a broad gravel track. Turn left.

4) This byway is part of the Stour Valley Walk. Follow the track between high hedges and patches of woodland for almost a mile before it opens on to a lane. Turn right. Follow this lane as it bends right, then turns sharp left downhill along another lane. At the base of the hill, the lane bends right then climbs into the village of Chartham.

5) Go straight across a crossroads. This lane drops into the watermeadows before crossing the Stour and climbing gently to reach the green. At the far side of the green bear right along the footpath through the churchyard.

Lying in the watermeadows are massive concrete tank traps left over from the Second World War. When it was feared that Hitler's panzers might land on the beaches of Kent, the roads leading inland were blocked with these defensive works. In most places they were removed at the end of the war, but here they were simply pushed to the side of the road and left. Perhaps the good folk of Chartham are hanging on to them in case another invader from Europe should loom into view.

Chartham Church is worth a visit, though it is open only on Sundays and summer afternoons. The wooden roof dates back over 600 years and is one of the finest in Kent, while the brasses are particularly fine. These days, of course, brass rubbers are not allowed to touch the original tombs, but replicas are to hand in the nave and rubbing of them is encouraged.

The mill beside the Great Stour, where the path crosses this river for the first time.

6) At the far side of the churchyard turn right, then almost immediately left along a surfaced towpath beside the Great Stour. About half a mile along

the riverside path a cluster of buildings on the far bank is the hamlet of Horton.

Horton is now little more than a small group of houses and a farm beside Chartham, but time was when it was an independent settlement of its own. The manor of Horton was always small, and never wealthy, but it was distinct. It was owned by the monastery of Christ Church, Canterbury. The monks saw no reason to keep a vicar installed at Horton, and instead sent a monk out to preach sermons and conduct services as necessary. The little chapel that ministered to the folk of Horton fell into disuse during the 17th century and was converted into a barn, later falling into ruin and is now little more than a heap of stones.

If local rumour is to be believed, however, there is rather more left of the old Horton Chapel than a few tumbled stones. A strange, grey shape has been seen walking along the Great Stour hereabouts. It is said to be one of the monks sent here to minister to the flock. The phantom monk is not seen often and even then not very clearly. Perhaps after all these years he is fading from the mortal world as some ghosts have a habit of doing. Or, as some cynics suggest, he might just be a patch of mist rising from the Stour.

7) Continue along the riverside walk, now no longer surfaced, as it crosses fields and passes open ponds, always keeping the river close on your right. The path eventually emerges on to the A28 over a stile next to a five bar gate. Turn left to cross the railway, then take the first right into Howfield Lane. Almost immediately you will find Howfield Manor Hotel on the right.

The broad track through the woodland beyond the mill that leads to the mysterious prehistoric burial mound and its supernatural inhabitants.

The Manor is built on land that was once a small monastery, the residents of which farmed the hills and prayed for the souls of the local yeomen and their families.

The story goes that each night a monk was given the task of staying awake to watch the time and call his brothers to prayer at the appropriate moment for their religious offices. This particular night the brother on watch fell asleep, allowing a candle to topple over and set fire to the buildings. He was roused from his sleep only when it was too late to save the little monastery. Realising the danger to his fellow monks, the hapless man raced into the burning building to rescue them, unaware that they had already fled the conflagration and were hurrying down to the Stour to collect water in buckets for a vain attempt at quenching the flames. The distraught monk who had fallen asleep died in the flames, which no amount of water from the Stour could put out.

The little monastery was too small to be worth rebuilding, so the lands passed to the Church. At the reformation they were sold to secular landlords and, in time, Howfield Manor

was built on the site. The current building dates largely from Victorian times, but that has done nothing to stop the phantom of the monk who failed in his duty from returning to wander around the site of his old home. It has been reported that, now and then, the faint sound of chanting and singing has been heard here, but it is the solitary monk who is the more frequent visitor.

For part of its length, the Chilham walk follows one of the well signed paths laid out by Kent Council.

8) Continue uphill along Howfield Lane to reach the little village of Chartham Hatch. As the lane bends right, turn left downhill past some houses and out of the village. At a T-junction turn left, then almost immediately right into what appears to be the private drive of a house. This is, in fact, a section of the North Downs Way. Persist in walking along the gravel drive behind the house, through a gateway, and you will find a sign for the North Downs Way pointing along the edge of a field towards a wood-crowned hill.

9) Follow the well-signed North Downs Way as it skirts these woods, then joins a lane that carries it back under the railway. Immediately past the railway, turn right off the lane to follow the North Downs Way through an orchard and up a hill. The route then turns left to skirt an open field, before turning right and dropping sharply down into a blind valley. Climbing the other side of the valley, the route skirts a small

Tank traps from the Second World War mark the entrance to Chartham.

wood to the right, then enters a long, gloomy avenue of trees.

10) At the far end of the avenue, the North Downs Way enters a lane by way of a small gate. Cross the lane and walk along a lane with houses on both sides. At the end of this short lane, turn right to enter the village of Old Wives Lees. In the centre of the village is a five-ways road junction. Take the second left, leading down a gentle slope that suddenly becomes much steeper after the lane takes a left hand turn. At the base of the hill go straight across a crossroads and almost at once you emerge on to the A252. Cross the main road with care, then continue straight on and uphill to return to the central square of Chilham.

The ghost of Horton is said to resemble a monk, indicating his possible identity.

The gates to Howfield Manor Hotel, where a fatal tragedy from centuries gone by has its ghostly echoes.

The gloomy avenue that carries the North Downs Way into the village of Old Wives Lees.

The route from Old Wives Lees down to Chilham is a steep and winding lane.

Walk No.14
Romney Marsh

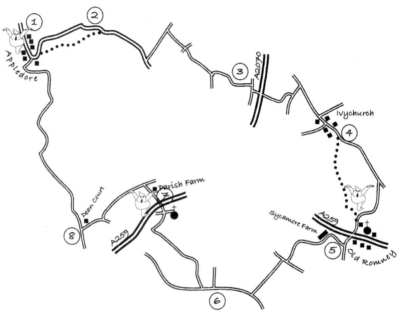

The new village sign for Appledore commemorates the fruit trees that thrive hereabouts.

Romney Marsh

Distance:	**16 miles**
Ghostly Rating:	* * *
Route:	**Appledore - Ivychurch - Old Romney - Brookland - Appledore**
Map:	**OS Explorer 125**
Start/Parking:	**Appledore high street.**
Public Transport:	**Appledore Railway Station and level crossing are on the walk at Point 2.**
Conditions:	**This route is mostly over lanes and surfaced paths.**
Refreshments:	**There are pubs at Appledore, Ivychurch and Old Romney that offer meals and a shop in Appledore that sells soft drinks, crisps and snacks.**

This is the longest walk in the book, but is over the flat Romney Marsh where no steep hills offer problems. It is a gentle stroll, although a long one. The ghosts are a mixed bag, but hark back to the history of this surprisingly remote and windswept area of Kent.

The Walk

1) Park in the high street of Appledore, and walk south towards the church.

This area of the village is haunted by a boisterous group of ghosts. These four young men wear the ill-fitting khaki uniforms of World War II infantry with, for those close enough to see such detail, the flash "CANADA" on their shoulders. They seem jovial enough as they stroll around the village, laughing and joking with each other, but paying no attention to the modern world around them.

These four men came to Appledore in the summer of 1942 from their homes in Canada. Like many other brave young men from Canada they had come to Britain to help our nation defy the armed might of Nazi Germany. Their stay here was to be short and happy, but was to end in tragedy. Along with the rest of their unit they were billeted in Appledore so as to be close to the South Coast and ready for the mission in which they were to take part.

During 1941 and early 1942 a series of highly successful raids on the coasts of occupied Europe had been made by commandoes and other units. It had been decided to follow these up with a major raid. This raid had a dual purpose, on the one hand it was to destroy a major port and so deny its facilities to the Germans, on the other it was to test the

The high street of Appledore is the scene for some boisterous fun by the local ghosts.

feasibility of capturing a port intact. The acquisition of a port would be vital to supply any future invasion of occupied France, as eventually took place on D-Day in 1944. The target port for the raid was Dieppe.

In the weeks before the raid the Canadians staying in Appledore became popular. Their easy going manners and cheerful good humour made them good companions, and they always paid their way. Then, in August, the Canadians marched away to raid Dieppe. Due to poor planning by the Allies and quick responses by the Germans, the raid was a disaster. Several of the Canadian units that took part were effectively wiped out – every single man being killed or captured.

Soon after news of the massacre reached Appledore these four soldiers began to appear in spectral form. At first people took them for other soldiers, but none were staying in the village. Laughing, joking and larking about the men seem to be recreating their last happy days on Earth before they went off to meet death in battle.

2) Follow the high street south to cross the canal. Turn sharp left, taking the path that runs across fields beside the road to reach the level crossing where the road crosses the railway at Appledore Station. Beyond the station take the first left, Arrowhead Lane, then the first right. Follow this lane south to a T-junction.

3) At the T-junction turn right then immediately left. This lane brings you to the A2070. Cross the main road and continue along the lane to a T-junction. Turn left, then right to enter the village of Ivychurch.

4) Beyond Ivychurch turn off the lane to join a footpath running across the open fields to Old Romney. The path joins a lane just before it enters Old Romney. Turn right to pass the church on your left as you reach the A259.

The footpath from Ivychurch to Old Romney runs beside an overgrown stream.

It is around here that several walkers have reported a most unnerving experience. They hear what seems to be the steady drone of an aircraft engine. But no aircraft can be seen overhead that might account for the sound, even on clear and cloudless days. Gradually the noise gets louder, as if the aircraft is approaching from the south. Suddenly the engines take on a sound of urgency as they surge with power. The volume increases dramatically as if the aircraft is diving at speed.

The fields around Old Romney are the scene for a very noisy ghost, though it is never seen.

Still nothing is to be seen in the skies above.

As the screaming engines reach a crescendo of volume, the jagged sounds of tearing metal and chattering guns rip through the air. Louder and louder the sounds become as if the invisible aircraft is about to appear just feet away. And then all is silent.

The sounds are gone.

It is thought that these fearsome noises are the ghostly echoes of a German bomber that was shot down here, and all the crew killed, during the Battle of Britain in 1940.

5) Cross the A259 and then turn right along a lane that bends left in front of Sycamore Farm. This lane ends at a T-junction. Turn right, then left.

6) At another T-junction turn right, then take the second turning on the right and follow this lane into Brookland. Pass the church and head northwest to reach a small roundabout.

This marks the spot where a gallows formerly stood. The remote and insular Romney Marsh was for many years a major centre for smuggling. During the 18th century, when import taxes on brandy, lace and other luxuries was especially high, the folk of the Marsh earned a good living by bringing such items in illegally from France. With miles of coast for the authorities to watch and a thousand hiding places in the Marsh where goods might be stored, this was ideal smuggling territory.

The church tower at Brookland is of an unusual design.

The site of the old gibbet outside Brookland is the site of some odd goings-on.

The authorities could not hope to catch every consignment of smuggled goods, so they adopted a policy of intimidation instead. Any smugglers who were caught were hanged here, in the centre of the marsh where their dangling bodies could be seen by all and, it was hoped, act as a deterrent.

It is one of these unfortunates whose ghost returns to pace restlessly around the spot where he died and where his body was left to hang for weeks. Some motorists have taken the phantom for a man waiting to cross the road and have slowed down, only for him to vanish mysteriously.

7) Cross the main road and walk past Parish Farm to a T-junction. Turn left. At a second T-junction turn right.

8) This lane reaches a T-junction beside Dean Court. Turn right. Follow this long, winding lane northward across the bleak landscape of Romney Marsh to return to the canal bridge at Appledore.

The bleak landscape of Romney Marsh offers little shelter from sun, rain or wind. It is well to come prepared for this lengthy walk.